GIFTED STUDENTS
in Primary Schools
Differentiating the Curriculum

GIFTED STUDENTS
in Primary Schools

Differentiating the Curriculum

MIRACA U. M. GROSS
BRONWYN MACLEOD
DIANA DRUMMOND
CAROLINE MERRICK

A GERRIC PUBLICATION
The University of New South Wales
Sydney

About the cover
Gifted and talented children are a country's greatest natural resource. The use of images from nature to highlight the covers of the GERRIC series of gifted education resources reminds us of this.

Published in Australia by
Gifted Education Research, Resource and Information Centre (GERRIC)
The University of New South Wales, Sydney
UNSW NSW 2052
Australia

Telephone: 02 9385 1972
Facsimile: 02 9385 1973
E-mail: gerric@unsw.edu.au
Web: www.arts.unsw.edu.au/gerric

Published in association with
INSCRIPT Publishing, Australia
E-mail: info@inscript.com.au
Web: www.inscript.com.au

Commissioning Editor: Miraca U. M. Gross
Managing Editor: Rosalind Walsh Elder
Publisher: Richard Stanford
Editor: William Pearce
Design: INSCRIPT Publishing
Photography: Steve Walsh

First published in 2001
Reprinted 2003, 2005

Copyright © 2003 Gifted Education Research, Resource and Information Centre (GERRIC)
The University of New South Wales, Sydney

All rights reserved. No part of this publication may be reproduced, stored in a retrieval system, or transmitted in any form or by any means, electronic or mechanical, including photocopying, recording or otherwise, without the prior written permission of the Gifted Education Research, Resource and Information Centre (GERRIC), The University of New South Wales.

National Library of Australia
Cataloguing-in-Publication data:

Gross, Miraca U. M.
Gifted Students in Primary Schools: Differentiating the Curriculum

Bibliography.
ISBN 0 7334 1824 4

1. Gifted children – Education – Australia
2. Gifted children – Education (Primary) – Australia
3. Gifted children – Education (Primary) – Australia – Curricula
I. MacLeod, Bronwyn. II. The University of New South Wales, Gifted Education Research, Resource and Information Centre (GERRIC). III. Title.

Printed in Australia by Ligare Pty Ltd

This book is dedicated to the memory of

Leta Stetter Hollingworth
(1886–1939)
an early and passionate advocate of accelerative
enrichment for gifted primary students

and, with love, to our families

John Gross,
David and Lauren Easton,
Charles and Sophie Drummond,
Bradley, Cameron and Daniel Merrick.

ACKNOWLEDGMENTS

A book such as this is not possible without the efforts of many people. We thank the following principals, teachers and schools for their support and dedication to the writing of this book:

MLC School, Burwood, NSW
Principal: Barbara Stone

St Catherine's, Waverley, NSW
Junior School Principal: Denice Scala
Teachers:
M. Davidson (unit on page 66)
D. Kempe (unit on page 66)
J. McLean (unit on page 66)
J. Lightfoot (unit on page 67)
C. Salvo (unit on page 67)
R. Compor (unit on page 68)
K. Haining (unit on page 68)

Individual teachers
Lori Koplik, Rhode Island, USA (unit on pages 79–84)
Cheryl Gherardini, Rhode Island, USA (unit on pages 79–84)
Deborah Gaulin in the Schools of California Online Resources for Educators (SCORE) Project (unit on pages 111–118)
Sue Floro, Oatlands, NSW (unit on page 120)

CONTENTS

CHAPTER 1	Conceptions of Giftedness and Talent	1
CHAPTER 2	Characteristics of Gifted Students	9
CHAPTER 3	Off-Level Testing and Curriculum Compacting	19
CHAPTER 4	Principles of Curriculum Development	33
CHAPTER 5	Models of Curriculum Development — Maker	39
CHAPTER 6	Models of Curriculum Development — Bloom/Krathwohl	51
CHAPTER 7	Models of Curriculum Development — Kaplan	61
CHAPTER 8	Models of Curriculum Development — Williams	69
CHAPTER 9	Independent Research Projects	75
CHAPTER 10	Developing Units of Work	85
CHAPTER 11	Evaluating Units of Work	93
CHAPTER 12	Putting It All Together: Examples of Units of Work	101
CHAPTER 13	More Sample Activities	119
CHAPTER 14	The Harry Potter Series — Gross	129
APPENDIX	Pro-forma Models, Checklists and Glossary of Acronyms	139
REFERENCES		159

CHAPTER 1
CONCEPTIONS OF GIFTEDNESS AND TALENT

hat do the terms 'gifted' and 'talented' mean? Are they synonymous or do they indicate different qualities? Are there varying levels of giftedness and talent? Why do these questions create so much debate amongst those responsible for the education of gifted and talented students?

These are important questions, because the definition of giftedness or talent which a school adopts will influence both the identification procedures it will use and the curricula and programs that will be developed to respond to students who will be identified.

Before developing or using curriculum strategies with gifted students, schools should decide on the definition or model of giftedness which they will adopt and work from. This model should be accepted and utilised by all educators involved, as well as the school community as a whole.

Early definitions of giftedness and talent focused primarily on high intelligence. Later definitions broadened the view of giftedness to include many domains of ability. The timeline that follows is a brief overview of the developments of definitions since that of Galton in 1869.

CHAPTER 1

A TIMELINE OF DEVELOPMENT

Definitions of giftedness

Year	Author	Definition
1869	Galton	Intelligence is related to 'keen' senses and is largely hereditary.
1905	Binet	Introduced the idea of 'mental age'; created the first structured intelligence test.
1930	Terman	Gifted children are high achievers, find learning easy, and are usually physically and emotionally healthier than children of average ability.
1940	Witty	Gifted children may show remarkable performance in any potentially valuable field.
1957	DeHaan and Havighurst	Gifted children show unusual promise in some socially useful area.
1960	Sumption and Luecking	Gifted children possess a superior nervous system and are characterised by the ability to perform tasks which require a high degree of intellectual abstraction or creative imagination.
1972	Marland	Gifted children possess outstanding abilities, and are capable of high performance in the areas of general intellectual and/or specific academic ability; creative/productive thinking; leadership; visual and performing arts; psychomotor ability.
1978	Renzulli	Developed the 'Three-Ring Conception of Giftedness': the interaction between above average general intelligence; high levels of task commitment; and high levels of creativity.
1981	Sternberg	Developed the 'Triarchic Theory of Intelligence': the relationship between environment; experience; and information processing capabilities.
1982	Gardner	Developed the 'Theory of Multiple Intelligences': linguistic; musical; logical-mathematical; spatial; bodily kinesthetic; the ability to notice and make distinctions among individuals; access one's own feelings about life.
1983	Tannenbaum	Developed the 'Psychosocial Definition of Giftedness': giftedness = potential; talent = developed abilities. Five factors interact: general ability, special ability, nonintellective factors, environmental and chance factors.
1985	Gagné	Developed the 'Differentiated Model of Giftedness and Talent': the child progresses from giftedness (high potential) to talent (high performance) through the learning process, assisted by intrapersonal and environmental factors.
1986	Feldhusen	Giftedness is a synthesis of general intellectual ability; positive self-concept; achievement motivation; and talent.

A closer look ...

As can be seen, while conceptions of giftedness have broadened considerably over the last 100 years, they share three important common elements:
- Gifted children have the *potential* for unusually high performance in at least one area.
- The capacity to think clearly, analytically and evaluatively is a prerequisite for high performance in any area.
- The cream does not automatically rise to the top. The child's personality and environment can help or hinder the translation of potential into performance.

During the last century there was a continual development and refinement of definitions of giftedness. Terman (1926), DeHaan and Havighurst (1957), Marland (1972), Renzulli (1978), Tannenbaum (1983) and Gagné (1985), among others, have presented models to explain their definition of giftedness.

Terman

It is often believed that Lewis Terman *defined* gifted learners as those who scored in the top 1 per cent of the population on general intellectual ability. However, although the study for which Terman is most famous focused on a longitudinal study of 1528 children whose IQ scores were above 140, he did not define giftedness as a specific IQ score or percentage of the population.

Terman's study showed that while the majority of gifted students experienced success at school, many were still required to work, in the classroom, at levels far below their capacity. In general, however, his sample were happy, well-adjusted children who achieved high levels of success in their adult lives.

DeHaan and Havighurst and The Marland Report

DeHaan and Havighurst (1957) defined gifted children as those who show unusual promise in some socially useful area and whose talents might be brought to fulfilment through appropriate educational programs.

Their definition was followed by a very similar statement by Sidney Marland, the United States Commissioner for Education (1972), which defined gifted and talented children as those identified by professionally qualified persons, who by virtue of outstanding abilities are capable of high levels of performance. Children capable of high levels of performance included those with demonstrated achievement and/or potential ability in any of the following areas, singly or in combination:
- **General intellectual ability** was usually defined in terms of a high intelligence test score — generally two standard deviations above the mean — on individual or group measures. Parents and teachers often recognise students with general intellectual talent by their wide-ranging fund of general information and high levels of vocabulary, memory, abstract word knowledge, and abstract reasoning.
- **Specific academic aptitude.** Students with specific academic aptitudes were those who displayed outstanding potential or performance (at the 97th percentile or higher) on an achievement or aptitude test in a specific academic subject area such as mathematics or language arts.
- **Creative or productive thinking.** This is the ability to produce new or original ideas by bringing together elements usually thought of as independent or dissimilar, and the aptitude for developing new meanings that have social value. Characteristics of creative and productive students include openness to experience, setting personal standards for evaluation, ability to play with ideas, willingness to take risks, preference for complexity, tolerance for ambiguity, positive self-image, and the ability to become absorbed in a task.

- **Leadership ability.** Leadership can be defined as the ability to direct individuals or groups to a common decision or action. Students who demonstrate giftedness in leadership ability use group skills and negotiate effectively in difficult situations. Many teachers recognise leadership through a student's keen interest and skill in problem solving. Leadership characteristics include self-confidence, responsibility, cooperation, and the ability to adapt readily to new situations.
- **Visual and performing arts.** Students gifted in the visual and performing arts have the potential for high levels of performance in visual art, music, dance, drama, or other related studies.
- **Psychomotor ability.** (This was later removed from the definition.) Students gifted with superior psychomotor abilities have the potential for unusual success in areas of physical performance such as sport and athletics.

Renzulli

Joseph Renzulli (1978) developed a 'three-ring' definition of giftedness proposing that giftedness was the interaction between three basic clusters of human traits. These traits were detailed as above-average general ability, high levels of task commitment, and high levels of creativity. 'Gifted and talented children are those possessing or capable of developing this composite set of traits and applying them to any potentially valuable area of human performance' (Renzulli, 1978, p. 261).

This definition, however, is felt by many people working in gifted education to disallow the presence of the gifted underachiever, who is rarely described as 'task-committed' (Gagné, 1985; Jarrell and Borland, 1990; Gross, 1993). Furthermore, many fields of performance do not require the element of creativity.

Tannenbaum

Previous definitions concentrated on the ability and achievements of gifted children, but did not recognise the importance of environmental influences. Abraham Tannenbaum, on the other hand, proposed that giftedness should be regarded as: 'an extraordinary promise for productivity or performance in areas of work that are publicly prized' (Tannenbaum, 1983, p. 89) and argued that along with general and specific abilities, a gifted child also needs facilitative personal attributes and experiences within a fostering environment for talent to emerge. His definition implies the separation between 'promise' or potential and 'performance' or talent. Tannenbaum's model describes the internal requirements and external events which act upon potential to produce excellence in performance.

Gagné

The model of Françoys Gagné, first developed in 1985, provides a diagrammatic representation of the link between promise and fulfilment, or potential and performance, but sets the factors of personality and environment in a somewhat different relationship to those of aptitude or ability, than does Tannenbaum.

Gagné argues that the terms giftedness and talent should not be used synonymously, and he proposes a most useful distinction: 'Giftedness corresponds to competence which is distinctly above average in one or more domains of ability. Talent refers to performance which is distinctly above average in one or more fields of human performance' (Gagné, 1985, p. 108).

A student can be *gifted* — that is, possess aptitude, competence, or potential significantly beyond that expected for his or her age in any one of several domains of human ability or, for that matter, in all of them. Gagné suggests four major domains: intellectual, creative, socio-affective and sensorimotor.

GAGNÉ'S DIFFERENTIATED MODEL OF GIFTEDNESS AND TALENT

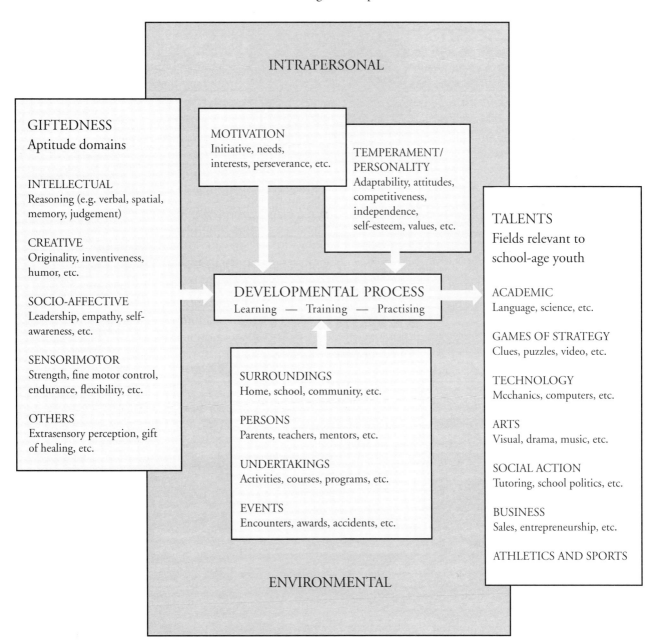

Reproduced by permission

Unlike Renzulli, Gagné separates the domains of intellectual and creative ability; it is not necessary, under this definition, for a child to possess high potential in both these domains in order to be acknowledged as gifted.

The gifted student may become *talented* — that is, demonstrate superior performance or achievement, in any one, or many, of a multiplicity of talent fields. Gagné emphasises that specific talents may develop from the intertwining of abilities from several different domains. In music, for example, the skilled composer–performer may draw on abilities from the cognitive, creative, socio-affective and sensorimotor domains. He further demonstrates that excellence in many fields of performance, for example, computer science, requires the interweaving of several quite different talents.

Within Gagné's definition, a child can be *gifted* (possessing unusually high potential) without being *talented* (displaying unusually high levels of performance). To explain the relationship between the two, he places in the centre of his model a cluster of catalytic variables which can either facilitate or impede the translation of giftedness into talent.

Crucial to the process of talent development is the quality of the student's learning, training or practice (Gagné, 1995). Impinging on this process, however, are personality factors in the individual student. Motivation, while not a necessary ingredient of giftedness as Renzulli proposed, is certainly essential if the child is to develop as talented. Students must have the motivation to get started, the motivation to apply themselves and the motivation to persevere when the going gets tough! They must also have a high degree of self-confidence and healthy self-esteem, and must accept and value their own gifts. Too often conceit, which we naturally want children to avoid, is confused with a healthy pride in one's abilities, which is an essential constituent of self-esteem. The gifted student must feel good about being gifted.

Also affecting the process of learning, training and practice are a number of environmental variables such as the quality of the teaching and parenting the student receives, the provisions the school makes, or fails to make, to develop gifts into talents, and even the social ethos of the community which, can dictate which talents are valued and, consequently, which programs of talent development will be established or funded. Gagné shows how a supportive environment can enhance not only the student's likelihood of academic success, but also the development of a strong and healthy personality.

Gagné's model gives definitions of giftedness and talent which are solidly grounded in research on human abilities and which demonstrate in a practical way, the links between aptitude and achievement. Gifts are natural innate abilities, while talents are systematically developed skills. This model recognises the student who may have high ability but who may be underachieving, demotivated, or prevented from realising his or her potential by environmental, personality or physiological constraints. In other words, a child can be gifted, but not yet talented. The teacher's task, and challenge, is to recognise the gift and foster the talent.

Gagné's model has gained wide acceptance in Australia. It is practical, teacher-friendly, and recognises the student who may be gifted in a single subject area, as well as those who have several gifts.

This book is designed to assist individual teachers to develop a differentiated curriculum for students gifted in specific subjects, or to assist teaching teams to develop a differentiated program for students who are gifted in several areas. We have, therefore, adopted Gagné's model as the definition of giftedness which underpins this book. The book is also designed to assist teachers to respond both to underachieving gifted students who need academic challenge to encourage the development of their potential, and to talented students who are already achieving successfully and who need to be presented with work commensurate with their level of achievement.

Is everyone gifted or talented?

During the early 1980s a small minority of Australian educators vigorously promoted the view that every child has gifts or talents. This stance was motivated by socio-political intentions rather than educational concerns. Abraham Tannenbaum, speaking at an education conference in Adelaide, humorously but logically refuted the premise:

> Unfortunately there are still some people who accept a pseudoscientific belief that the human mind consists of many discrete abilities, and that if you break down these independent abilities and keep on breaking them down, you will eventually reach a point where there are more special aptitudes than there are people walking on the face of the earth. And the logical conclusion and absurdity that arises from this belief is the idea that if there are more aptitudes around than people, then surely each human being must have a chance of possessing at least one superior aptitude. Sadly, however, this is not so. God was not a democrat when She distributed abilities.
> (Tannenbaum, 1988)

Tannenbaum was affirming that human abilities are not, as is sometimes claimed, discrete or only tenuously linked. For example, mathematical ability and musical ability are not two separate 'intelligences' as proposed by Gardner (1983) in his theory of 'multiple intelligences' — they are *aptitudes* which teachers of maths and teachers of music happily acknowledge to be quite strongly correlated. Any psychiatrist will affirm that what Gardner calls 'inter-personal intelligence' — the capacity to understand other people — is closely related to what he calls 'intra-personal intelligence' — the capacity to understand oneself — and that indeed a high correlation between the two is essential for mental health. 'Politically incorrect' though it may be, we have to acknowledge that students who achieve highly in one area quite often have the *potential* for high achievement in several areas. We need to look for, and foster, these additional gifts.

It is necessary to distinguish between *gifts* and *strengths*. Every student has an individual *strength* — something that stands out as a high point relative to his or her other abilities. For Kate, a Year 4 student whose level of language skills is several years below that appropriate to her chronological age, the capacity to work in maths at a level appropriate to her age may be a much-valued strength. Kate's teachers will identify and foster this strength while they are working to help her remediate her weaknesses in language.

However, to say that Kate has a *gift* for maths, she would have to have the potential to perform at a level significantly beyond what we would expect of most Year 4 students. If she were mathematically *talented* she would already be performing at a level well beyond her peers. And Kate isn't doing that. Her maths abilities and achievements lie well within the normal range for students of her age. Maths is her area of special strength, but she isn't mathematically gifted.

The Year 4 maths curriculum has been developed in response to Kate's levels of mathematical aptitudes and to her maths learning needs. However, if she were mathematically gifted or talented she would require something rather more — a curriculum quite substantially differentiated in terms of its level, its pace, its content and its level of abstraction.

Every student has individual strengths and it is important that we identify and foster these strengths in all our students. But for some — a minority — these strengths are of such an order that they can justifiably be called gifts, and for these students the pace, level and content of the regular curriculum may be seriously inadequate.

Few teachers in Australia still view gifted and talented children as rarities — the top 1 or 2 per cent of the population. Over the last twenty years a more realistic perception of the prevalence of giftedness and talent has emerged. Françoys Gagné suggests that we should view around 15 per cent of students in any subject area as being gifted in that subject. Even when we acknowledge the 'overlap' — students who are gifted in more than one area — that's a lot of gifted and talented young people!

However, the broader we take our definition, the more we have to acknowledge that there are levels or degrees of giftedness. Our colleagues working in other areas of special education — teachers of hearing impaired, intellectually disabled or autistic children, for example — recognise that there are different levels of these conditions, and that the intervention that is designed for a particular child must respond not only to the presence of the condition, but to the degree to which it affects the child. For example, interventions developed for students with moderate hearing impairment are of little use with students whose hearing impairment is severe.

Similarly, we have to acknowledge that gifted children are not a homogeneous group. There are different levels, as well as different kinds, of giftedness. Highly and exceptionally gifted students need a curriculum that is even more challenging and intellectually rigorous than their moderately gifted classmates.

In order to identify a gifted child, it is important to understand the variety of characteristics which act as pointers towards or indicators of giftedness. All of these characteristics do not necessarily need to be present for a child to be identified as gifted, and some may be more readily observable than others. The following pages describe these characteristics, their positive and negative manifestations in the classroom, and their implications for classroom teachers.

CHAPTER 2
CHARACTERISTICS OF GIFTED STUDENTS

COGNITIVE AND AFFECTIVE CHARACTERISTICS OF GIFTED LEARNERS

ifted learners often possess a heightened level of curiosity; a fascination with seeking out and acquiring new knowledge; a wide variety of interests; power of concentration; superior reasoning powers and ability to handle abstract ideas; flexibility in thinking and considering problems from a number of viewpoints; and, an alert and subtle sense of humour (Clark, 1983; Baska, 1989; Gross, 1994).

Gifted learners often develop at an early age the ability to delay closure — simple, immediately obvious responses are unlikely to satisfy them; an ability to handle abstractions; superiority in quality and quantity of written and/or spoken vocabulary; interest in the subtleties of words and their uses; the desire to read and absorb books written for an audience well beyond their years; and, the ability to learn and recall important details, concepts and principles (Hollingworth, 1926; Tannenbaum, 1983; Clarke, 1983).

Gifted learners often learn quickly and easily and retain what is comprehended; grasp mathematical concepts readily; show creative ability or imaginative expression in such areas as music, art, dance and drama; show sensitivity and finesse in rhythm, movement, and bodily control; show outstanding responsibility and independence in classroom work; set realistically high standards for themselves; are self-critical in evaluating and correcting their own efforts; show initiative and originality in intellectual work; show social poise and an ability to communicate with adults in a mature way; and, get excitement and pleasure from intellectual challenge.

However, other characteristics which many gifted children possess are less easily understood by their classmates, or even by the children themselves. These include:
- over-responsiveness to intellectual or emotional stimulus: other children may find it hard to understand why the gifted student becomes so passionate about things;
- perceptiveness: early development of the ability to 'read between the lines' of other people's words or actions;
- empathy: an unusual capacity to understand how other people feel;
- sensitivity: a tendency to take criticism very much to heart;
- entelechy: extraordinary degrees of motivation — a single-minded pursuit of goals, particularly the drive to develop one's potential to the fullest.

(Torrance, 1965; Lovecky, 1986; Silverman, 1993)

It is those social-emotional traits, even more than the cognitive traits listed above, that alert students to the fact that their gifted age-peers are 'different' — and this difference may cause the gifted student to be distrusted or resented.

The effectiveness of teacher identification of gifted and talented students can be greatly enhanced by the use of trait lists which have been designed by researchers who are trained in both gifted education and psychological measurement. A particularly effective trait list for teachers in the early years of primary school is *Things This Young Child Has Done*, developed by Professor Micheal Sayler and included in the appendices of this book. This is a practical guided checklist of cognitive and affective behaviours which often indicate advanced intellectual development.

The traits and characteristics listed above are easy for teachers to recognise when they are manifested through positive classroom behaviours. Often, however, the pace and level of work presented to gifted students does little to engage their interest in learning, and they may respond with behaviours which are negative or even frankly disruptive.

Table 1 (p. 12) demonstrates how these characteristics of gifted students may be reflected in the classroom in both positive and negative ways. When a gifted student displays negative behaviour, this is often a call for help or at least an indication that some intervention is needed. Often, appropriate intervention can transform negative behaviour to positive behaviour. This allows for a more productive learning environment for all concerned!

Joyce VanTassel-Baska stresses that it is important to bear in mind the following points when considering the cognitive characteristics of gifted students:
- Not all children will display all of the characteristics.
- There will tend to be a range among gifted children in respect to each characteristic.
- These characteristics may be viewed as developmental.
- Some children may not display them at early stages of development but at later stages, while others may manifest the characteristics from a very early age.
- Characteristics of the gifted tend to cluster and thus constitute different profiles across children as the combination of characteristics varies.
- Characteristics may reveal themselves only when students engage in an area of interest and aptitude.

(VanTassel-Baska, 1996, p. 180)

Parent nominations

Primary school teachers have more opportunity to engage with and get to know their students than do their colleagues in secondary schools. In most cases, secondary school teachers see their students for less than six hours per week, and in general they see more than 100 students each day. Primary school teachers, by contrast, spend more than 25 hours each week with their students. They have so much more time to observe growth and change in these children. They can watch and assist the development of warm and supportive peer relationships. They can offer sustained comfort and understanding when things go wrong. They can support and model, throughout the day, the love of learning. They have more time for pastoral support. Nonetheless, primary school teachers who are not trained in gifted education may be far from expert identifiers of giftedness or talent in children. As we will discuss later in this chapter, research shows that parents are *far* more successful than untrained teachers.

Parents spend the best part of five years with their child before the school even becomes aware of the child's existence. They note their child's developmental milestones, they compare their child with what the baby books have led them to expect, they compare their child with other children in their district and in their own extended family and, later, they compare their child with others at pre-school. In the majority of cases they are very alert indeed to similarities and differences between their child and his or her age-peers.

Parents are able to note the ages at which the child moves through the stages of speech acquisition; the ages at which he or she starts to crawl, walk and run; the development of pre-reading skills or counting skills. *Teachers do not see these stages;* they have passed by the time we meet the child. Unless the parent actually tells us, we do not know when the child began to speak, the speed with which speech development progressed, the age at which the child began to walk; or the amount of sleep needed as a baby or a young child. Yet the early development of speech and movement, and a need for less sleep than is usual, are strong predictors of high intellectual ability in young children.

Parents of a gifted child, like other parents, compare their young child's development with that of age-peers and in most cases they become aware — sometimes very uncomfortably aware — that their child is different.

Numerous researchers have noted the early development of speech and movement which is typical of moderately gifted children (Terman, 1926; Witty, 1940; Tannenbaum, 1992). Whereas the average age at which a child can be expected to utter his or her first meaningful word is around twelve months (Staines and Mitchell, 1982), the gifted child begins to speak, on average, some two months earlier. Furthermore, the stages of speech acquisition are passed through earlier and with greater rapidity than in the child of average ability. By eighteen months the average child has a vocabulary of 3 to 50 words, but little attempt is made to link them into short phrases until the age of two; however, in gifted children, linking words into phrases can commence as early as twelve months. Jersild (1960) noted that, at the age of eighteen months, children of average ability were uttering a mean number of 1.2 words per 'remark', whereas their gifted age-peers were uttering 3.7 words per 'remark'. By the age of four the difference was even more remarkable; the mean number of words per 'remark' for average children was 4.6, while for the gifted children it was 9.5. All of this happens three years before the child enters school.

Studies of highly gifted children record instances of linguistic precocity far beyond even that of the moderately gifted children. The average age at which Australian children of IQ 160+, studied by Gross, uttered their first word was nine months. Several of these children spoke their first meaningful word (other than 'mamma-dadda' babble) by the age of six months (Gross, 1993).

CHAPTER 2

TABLE 1
CHARACTERISTICS OF GIFTED STUDENTS

CHARACTERISTICS	POSSIBLE NEGATIVE CLASSROOM BEHAVIOURS	SOME CLASSROOM NEEDS	RESULTANT POSITIVE CLASSROOM BEHAVIOURS
Heightened levels of curiosity and a wide variety of interests	Takes on too many projects; poor participant in group tasks; asks questions at inappropriate times; is easily diverted from the task; does not follow through on projects.	Exposure to a variety of subjects; opportunity to pursue individual interests; learning centres; individual educational programs; provision of open-ended tasks and creative and critical-thinking exercises; contact with experts.	Asks questions; investigates ideas; pays close attention and remembers things in great detail.
Long attention span	Dislikes interruptions and disruptive routines.	Long-term projects; individual education programs.	Learns to complete tasks.
Ability to handle abstract ideas	Questions others' ideas and may be seen as disrespectful.	Multidisciplinary units of work; theme-based work, e.g. change, social issues, global issues; higher levels of problem-solving.	Is able to make generalisations and test their validity; is aware of the consequences of his or her choices.
Flexibility in thinking	May be seen as disrespectful of authority; can be disruptive.	Exposure to creative and critical-thinking exercises.	Is able to solve problems using a wide range of strategies.
Alert and subtle sense of humour	May use humour at others' expense.	Opportunities to examine humour in positive and negative situations.	Uses humorous speech; tells 'funny' stories; understands 'adult' humour.
Superior vocabulary and verbal ability	May be 'bossy' and influence other students.	Foreign language studies; vocabulary-building exercises.	Is keen to participate in classroom discussions; peer leader; is able to conduct 'adult' conversations.
Advanced reading ability	Neglects other work and responsibilities; avoids interaction with peers.	Individualised and advanced reading program.	Reads widely; has advanced vocabulary and comprehension; is able to understand complex and abstract relationships.
Fast learner	Finishes quickly and becomes disruptive; 'showing off'.	Move beyond core curriculum; curriculum compacting; acceleration.	Learns the core content and skills quickly.
Excellent retention of knowledge	Attempts to control class.	Presentation of materials from memory; general knowledge exercises.	Has accurate recall of facts, details and events.

CHARACTERISTICS	POSSIBLE NEGATIVE CLASSROOM BEHAVIOURS	SOME CLASSROOM NEEDS	RESULTANT POSITIVE CLASSROOM BEHAVIOURS
Independent	Avoids discussions and group work; dislikes working with others; is uncooperative in group situations.	Independent study projects; development of organisational strategies; flexible timetabling; learning centres.	Develops research and study skills; presents and records work using multiple resources; is self-directed.
High level of personal responsibility and commitment	Frustration with personal performance — self-critical; perfectionism; frustration when working with others who do not meet his or her expectations.	Mentoring; develop goal-setting abilities; leadership opportunities; encouragement of intellectual risk-taking.	Is able to set realistic goals; learns self-acceptance; is tolerant of others; is an active and positive team member.
Strong feelings and opinions	Appears 'opinionated'; is argumentative; is overly sensitive to the opinions and behaviours of others.	Exposure to other viewpoints; problem-solving activities in the affective domain; discussion of values and morals; philosophy.	Is tolerant of other opinions and feelings; develops listening skills.
Advanced levels of moral judgement and sense of justice	Isolates self from peer group; frustration when attempting 'reforms'.	Discussion of value systems and levels of moral development; work in the affective domain.	Understands other value systems.
Preference for unusual, original and creative responses	Asks impertinent questions; does not accept the status quo; dislikes working in groups; is unorganised and absent-minded; finds decision-making difficult.	Mentoring; acceleration.	Asks curious questions; is a high achiever; participates in individual study programs; sees problems as a whole; thoughts and feelings are interconnected.
Immersion learner	Dislikes subject boundaries.	Individual educational programs.	Learns how to listen in a more focused way; synthesises material from different subjects.
Single-minded; does not accept the status quo	Appears bossy, stubborn, rebellious, unmotivated, inattentive, tactless and attention-seeking; is often teased by others; can become depressed as adolescent.	Mentoring; 'bibliotherapy'.	Develops a sense of 'real' self.
A high energy level; decreased need for sleep	Often difficult to live with; appears to be hyperactive; stimulus seekers; high need to explore the environment and seek new experiences; is easily bored without challenge.	Needs alternating activities requiring intellectual and creative stimulation with routine tasks.	Learns to use time to structure activities; learns to work individually.

(Adapted from Clark, 1983 and Baska, 1989)

The speech of some highly gifted children demonstrates quite remarkable fluency and complexity. Adam, one of Gross's subjects of IQ 160+, uttered his first word at five months and two months later was talking in three and four-word sentences. His mother recalls the astonishment of supermarket assistants as Adam, aged seven months, gave a running commentary on the grocery items as she wheeled him in the shopping trolley past the shelves. Peter, whose first word, spoken at eight months, was 'pussycat', surprised his parents at eighteen months by announcing, 'I think I'll have a quick shower'. Ian of IQ 200, knew all the words of the song *My Grandfather's Clock* by the age of 23 months.

Occasionally the speech of even quite highly gifted children may be delayed. In these situations, however, when speech does appear, it often arrives in the form of phrases or short sentences, rather than words in isolation. Robinson (1987) reports a young boy whose first utterance, at twenty months, was 'Look! Squirrel eating birds' food!'.

Just as highly gifted children generally demonstrate an unusually rapid progression through the stages of speech development, the development of mobility also tends to arrive early and to progress with unusual speed.

Even moderately gifted children learn to stand alone, walk and run earlier than their age-peers but highly gifted children display even greater precocity in movement. Silverman (1989) describes a girl of seven months who stood alone, climbed into chairs unassisted and went up and down stairs by herself. Gross (1993) describes Rick, of IQ 162, who was sitting up by himself at four months, running at eleven months and riding a bicycle unaided at age three. The mean age at which Gross's subjects of IQ 160+ sat up unsupported was six months, as opposed to seven to eight months in the general population. The mean age at which they walked while supported was ten months — one month earlier than the general population mean; and the mean age at which they were walking independently was twelve months — fully three months earlier than is usual. Not only do these gifted children become physically mobile at remarkably early ages, but the stages of skill development are traversed with exceptional speed.

Research has found that children who demonstrate a precocious development of speech and movement are highly likely to develop reading skills substantially earlier than their age-peers (Hollingworth, 1942; Gross, 1993). The research literature on highly gifted children contains a wealth of information on extremely gifted children who learned to read either with no assistance or with minimal assistance from their parents.

Research has consistently shown that parents are significantly more successful than teachers in identifying giftedness in the early childhood years (Jacobs, 1971; Ciha, Harris, Hoffman and Potter, 1974) particularly, as Robinson (1993) has pointed out, in domains such as the development of speech and movement, and the emergence of reading or literacy, where there are distinctive milestones and where strong normative expectations are held by the community.

Although some parents of gifted children do remain surprisingly unaware that their children are developmentally advanced, in most cases the onset of awareness that a child is 'different' occurs in the early childhood years. Robinson and Robinson (1992) reported that almost half of 550 young children aged from two to five years, who were 'volunteered' by their parents for a longitudinal study of high-ability children, and who were subsequently tested, had IQs of 132 or higher. This is statistically remarkable; only 2.3 per cent of the population scores at this level.

In general, parents of highly gifted children recognise their developmental precocity in the very early years (Silverman and Kearney, 1989; Gross, 1992, 1993; Morelock, 1994). More than 90 per cent of the parents of Gross's exceptionally and profoundly gifted children realised by their child's second birthday that the child was not only developmentally advanced, but remarkably so. Like the parents of highly gifted pre-

school children studied by Louis and Lewis (1992), Gross's parents cited an unusual facilitative and retentive memory, and an unusual capacity for abstract reasoning, as factors which signalled to them that their child might be gifted. However, they also reported that they had been alerted by the level of questioning, intense curiosity, desire to learn, and unusually advanced sense of humour displayed by the child, as well as the precocity of speech and movement and, in some cases, the spontaneous emergence of reading (Gross, 1993).

It is hardly surprising that parents are so much more successful than untrained teachers in identifying giftedness in the early years. It is during the early years of life that cognitive development proceeds most swiftly, and that the changes in the child's interactions with his or her environment are most visible, and most dramatic. By the time the teacher enters the scene, developmental changes have become more gradual. Furthermore, the parent sees a much wider range of cognitive and affective behaviours than does the teacher who, by the nature of things, operates in a setting which imposes greater uniformity of conduct upon the children in his or her charge. At home, gifted young children have no need to moderate their behaviour for peer or teacher acceptance. Highly gifted children may learn to camouflage their abilities within the first few weeks of school, to blend into the social conventions of the classroom.

As with teacher nomination, the reliability and validity of parent nomination can be greatly enhanced by training and the use of professionally developed trait lists. An excellent checklist for parents of children in the early years of school is *Things My Young Child Has Done*, developed by Professor Micheal Sayler as a companion to his teacher checklist discussed earlier and first published in Harrison (1995). It is also included in the Appendix of this book. This checklist asks parents to record examples of the development of speech, movement and reading in the young child, as well as several aspects of cognitive and affective development. Parents can take the completed checklist with them to their first meeting with the principal of the young child's school or preschool, or the child's prospective teacher. Indeed, many Australian schools now use this parent checklist as an integral part of their procedures to identify gifted and talented children.

A further checklist, also published in the Appendix of this book, is Sayler's *Things My Child Has Done*. This focuses on characteristics and behaviours of gifted children in the middle and upper years of primary school, and, like its 'younger sibling', allows parents to record illustrative aspects and incidents in their child's cognitive and affective development.

Smutney (1995) recommends that parents of gifted young children should also construct portfolios of their children's work, activities and interests, which will serve as a record of their intellectual development. 'A portfolio may include library book awards, preschool projects of merit, projects from home that are unusual, special awards from scouting or community service and video or audio-tapes of performances or projects (although photographs are better as they can be viewed at the time the portfolio is reviewed)' (Smutney, 1995, p. 15). Parents can take the portfolios to the children's future teachers before school starts, or as soon as possible after the school year begins, so that the teachers are not left to discover for themselves that the young children are exceptional, and before the children have the opportunity to discover for *themselves* that they are different, and respond by 'going underground'.

The portfolio technique can be particularly useful where a highly gifted child is already reading at an unusually advanced level, writing short stories or poetry, or creating exceptional artwork. Harrison (1998) and Winner (1996) have both documented truly remarkable examples of the artwork of highly gifted young children which demonstrate these children's astonishing visual memory and passion for detail. Teachers presented with such direct and unequivocal examples of precocity are less likely to suspect that the child's achievements are the result of parental 'hothousing'.

Parents of gifted and talented children can be an invaluable source of information about their child's development, and schools which properly view education as a partnership between the school, the home and the community cannot afford to ignore their experiences and insights.

Classroom implications

Regardless of the number of characteristics of giftedness possessed by a child or the intensity to which the characteristic is displayed, research (Maker, 1982; Passow, 1982; VanTassel-Baska, 1993; Gross, 1993) indicates that these must be addressed in the design of curriculum and learning experiences for these children. Joyce VanTassel-Baska (1988) also reports that three fundamental differences stand out from research on the characteristics of gifted students:
- the capacity to learn at faster rates;
- the capacity to find, solve and act on problems more readily;
- the capacity to manipulate abstract ideas and make connections.

Although gifted children differ within each of these points, it is clear that the curriculum for this group of students needs to allow time for in-depth exploration, manipulation of ideas and questions requiring higher order thinking, as well as acceleration when appropriate.

When planning learning experiences for students of lower academic ability, teachers generally agree that these students need a modified presentation of the core curriculum. Few would claim that it is either equitable or practical to expect these students to work at the same pace as students of average ability. Equally, the pace and level of curriculum must be modified for students with high ability.

To summarise, these following points should be remembered when planning curriculum experiences for students:

1. All learners should be provided with curriculum opportunities that allow them to attain optimal levels of learning.
2. Gifted learners have different learning needs compared with typical learners. Therefore, curriculum must be adapted or designed to accommodate these needs.
3. The needs of gifted learners cut across cognitive, affective, social and aesthetic areas of curriculum experiences.
4. Gifted learners are best served by a confluent approach that allows for both accelerated and enriched learning.
5. Curriculum experiences for gifted learners need to be carefully planned, written down, implemented, and evaluated in order to maximise potential effect.
(VanTassel-Baska, 1996, p. 126)

The recognition of some or all of the characteristics of a gifted student is an important stage in the identification process and is particularly important when the student may not be performing at the level indicated by his or her potential.

Often the identification of a gifted student will occur through the use of more than one method (multiple criteria identification). It is possible that information about a child may be offered to the school by the parents (such as the results of an independent psychologist's assessment); or the school counsellor may have assessed the child; or the school may have a policy of testing all students at some stage using a group intelligence test such as the Ravens Matrices.

These methods provide information concerning a student's ability and the possible levels of achievement they may be able to work towards. However, it is also important to realise that many of these gifted students will already know most of the work that is planned for their specific grade level. For example, a gifted student placed into a Year 3 class may very well know, and be proficient in, the majority of curriculum outcomes for this grade at the beginning of the school year.

The method known as 'off-level testing' may be used as an additional step in the identification process and will be discussed in the following chapter.

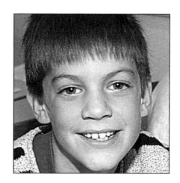

CHAPTER 3
OFF-LEVEL TESTING AND CURRICULUM COMPACTING

OFF-LEVEL TESTING

s early as 1917, Hollingworth, Garrison and Burke reported the need for above-level or 'off-level' tests with highly gifted children whose true abilities were not reflected in tests designed for their age. Research by Flanders (1987) on the scope and sequence of content and skills development in many of the mathematics textbooks used in schools showed that there is considerable duplication of work from year to year, particularly from Years 4 to 6. Gifted students may be required to mark time for several years, learning very little that they do not already know and having very little chance to show their true ability.

The effect often described as 'hitting the ceiling' of a test occurs when students may score highly in an age-appropriate test and yet not have the opportunity to display their full knowledge and capabilities. When this happens, it is clear that the level of difficulty of the particular test is not high enough and a test of greater difficulty is required. Gross describes the use of grade-level tests with highly gifted children as:

> ... a little like trying to measure the height of the Harlem Globetrotters on a pole which only goes up to 6 feet 6 inches, and then, when the coach protests that this won't tell him more than he can already see, defending our action by claiming that the pole we are using is a perfectly adequate measure for 99 percent of the population. (Gross, 1998a, p. 152)

The use of off-level tests allows teachers to place students in classes that are appropriate to their ability levels rather than simply age or grade-appropriate. Above-level tests may be developed by:
- giving to students, at the start of the year, a test of the material they will be expected to know at the end of the year;
- using a test designed for older students within the school;
- using already available tests such as competition papers, e.g. from The University of New South Wales Mathematics, Computer, English and Science competitions.

Alternatively, schools may choose to utilise the results from a talent search program, such as the Australian Primary Talent Search (APTS), as a means of determining appropriate curriculum and programming modifications for students who have undertaken this test. The goal of talent searches is to identify, through above-level testing, students who need further educational challenge to fully realise their potential.

Australian Primary Talent Search

The Australian Primary Talent Search was initiated by the Gifted Education Research, Resource and Information Centre (GERRIC) at The University of New South Wales, in association with the Belin-Blank International Centre for Gifted Education and Talent Development at The University of Iowa. It assesses academically gifted students in Years 3 to 6 on EXPLORE, a multiple-choice test developed by American College Testing as a test for 8th grade students. EXPLORE measures students' academic aptitude in four key learning areas: English, mathematics, reading comprehension and science reasoning.

Taking EXPLORE enables students to demonstrate unusual academic strengths in any or all of these four key learning areas by taking an academically challenging test at a level that is not generally set in primary school. Families receive two individualised score reports and a written interpretation of results. This interpretation guide includes recommendations for curriculum readiness. Families may choose to give the second copy of the report to their child's school.

To date, more than 5500 primary school students from around Australia have participated in APTS and the students' scores have been outstanding. The purpose of APTS testing is to see how students perform on an above-level test. Over 50 per cent of the Australian participants have scored higher than the average Year 8 student on one or more subject areas.

Of course, once gifted students have been identified through an off-level test, it is important that they are offered appropriate curricular options to ensure that their educational experience is challenging and rewarding.

CURRICULUM COMPACTING

Even after students have been identified by off-level testing as requiring a more advanced placement in a specific subject area, the core curriculum of this subject will contain much content that they have already mastered and further repetition will not be of any educational value. By compacting this curriculum, for example by reducing the core curriculum to only those skills or content areas that are not already mastered, these students are then able to participate in acceleration or enrichment activities to ensure they are still active participants in their learning process.

In summary, the rationale behind the process of compacting the curriculum may be listed as follows:

1. Students often already know most of a subject's content before 'learning it'.
2. The curriculum in many subjects has actually been 'dumbed down' in the past two to three decades.
3. The quality of curriculum materials and textbooks has failed to improve.
4. The needs of gifted and talented students are not often met in classrooms.
5. Compacting provides time for more challenging learning experiences and hence may enhance achievement levels.
6. The pace of instruction and practice time can be modified.
7. Compacting focuses on educational accountability.

(Chall and Conrad, 1991; Reis, Burns and Renzulli, 1992; Rogers, 1991)

In order to compact the curriculum, the learning objectives and outcomes of each topic within a subject need to be identified, the students pretested on these to establish any prior mastery, and finally an appropriate alternative program can be designed. Professor Karen Rogers of the University of St. Thomas has synthesised the following step by step process from a variety of sources, including Reis, Burns and Renzulli (1992), Starko (1986) and Winebrenner (1992).

The process

1. Identify the relevant learning objectives and outcomes in a subject area or topic. This may be achieved by asking several questions:
   - Do the objectives represent new learning?
   - Which objectives will equip students to use this content area?
   - Which objectives can be applied to the workplace?
   - Which objectives develop skills or concepts — not just facts?
   - Which objectives do gifted students need to understand?
   - Which objectives cannot be learned without formal or sustained instruction?
   - Which objectives reflect the priorities of the school or State department of education?

2. Find or develop a means of pretesting students on one or more of these objectives prior to instruction. Appropriate pretests may be:

CHAPTER 3

Objective-reference tests, for example:
- tests already published, e.g. with curriculum guide or text
- unpublished tests, e.g. developed by the teacher
- standardised, off-level 'achievement' tests
- standardised, off-level 'diagnostic' tests

Performance-based tasks, such as:
- oral tasks: discussions, brainstorming, recitations
- written tasks: brainstorming, essays, short-answer questions, concept maps
- manipulative tasks: puzzles, 'hands-on' tasks

3. Identify students who may benefit from curriculum compacting and should be pretested. The teacher can target students who:
   - consistently finish tasks quickly;
   - make careless mistakes;
   - appear bored during instruction time;
   - consistently daydream;
   - create their own distractions, e.g. games, puzzles and stories;
   - bring outside reading materials;
   - have a high level of performance in one or more areas;
   - test well despite average or below-average classwork;
   - ask advanced questions;
   - are sought by other students for assistance;
   - use an advanced vocabulary;
   - express interest in pursuing alternative or advanced topics;
   - will benefit based on the teacher's intuition and experience.

4. Pretest students to determine mastery levels of the chosen objectives and outcomes. A teacher may offer pretesting to all students by the following three possible alternatives:
   - **'Most difficult first' procedure** allows students to attempt the hardest level of the topic at the beginning of the work to 'buy' time for other interests.
   - **'Day One' pretest blitz**. Teacher prepares two parallel tests on the unit of work. All students attempt the first test and if mastery is displayed in any of the objectives, enrichment activities replace them. All students complete the post-unit test.
   - **'Day Three' pretest option**. Students are given the opportunity to 'test out' of a unit of work by completing a criterion referenced test or task on 'Day Three' after an accelerated presentation of the course on 'Day One' and 'Day Two'. Those who 'test out' begin working on long-term enrichment projects whilst the others begin a regular course of instruction.

5. Eliminate practice, drill or instructional time for students who have demonstrated mastery of these objectives and outcomes.

6. Streamline instruction of those objectives students have not yet mastered but are capable of mastering more quickly than their peers.

7. Offer enrichment or acceleration options for students whose curriculum has been compacted.

8. Keep records of this process and the instructional options available to 'compacted' students.

The following pages are examples of pretests used in the K-6 curriculum areas: Human Society and Its Environment (HSIE), Studies of Society and the Environment (SOSE), Mathematics, Science and Technology, and English.

CHAPTER 3

**EXAMPLE: PRETEST
HSIE/SOSE UNIT — STAGE 3 (YEARS 5 OR 6)
'GLOBAL ENVIRONMENTS'**

Section 1.

Look at the map of the world and answer the following questions.

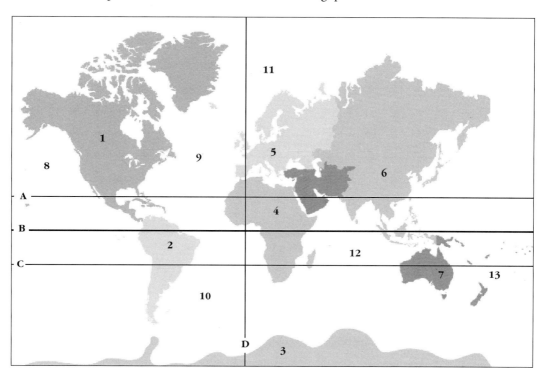

Provided by graphicmaps.com

- Name the continents marked on the map with the numbers:

    1. _____   5. _____
    2. _____   6. _____
    3. _____   7. _____
    4. _____

- Name the oceans marked on the map with the numbers:

    8. _____   11. _____
    9. _____   12 _____
    10. _____   13. _____

- Name the special lines marked on the map with the letters:

    A. _____   C. _____
    B. _____   D. _____

23

■ CHAPTER 3

Section 2.

Look at the map of Australia and answer the following questions.

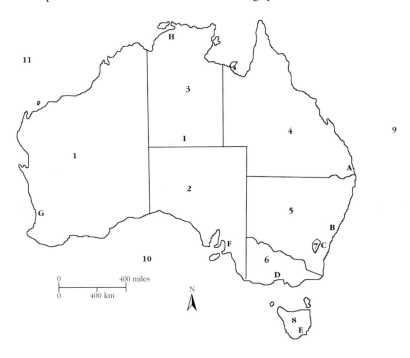

- Name the States and Territories shown by the numbers:

    1. _____   5. _____
    2. _____   6. _____
    3. _____   7. _____
    4. _____   8. _____

- Name the capital or major city marked with the letter:

    A. _____   F. _____
    B. _____   G. _____
    C. _____   H. _____
    D. _____   I. _____
    E. _____

- Name the oceans shown by the numbers:

    9. _____   11. _____
    10. _____

- Name and indicate on the map of Australia any other important geographical features.

    _____
    _____
    _____

Section 3.

Read the following sentences carefully and then mark each one either
T (True) or F (False):

1. A continent is a very large landmass. _____
2. A country is an area with several ruling governments. _____
3. The equator divides the world into two hemispheres. _____
4. Australia is west of the prime meridian. _____
5. The Murray River is in Western Australia. _____
6. Western Australia occupies the greatest area of Australia. _____
7. Tasmania is the second smallest Australian State. _____
8. The coastal strip in New South Wales is separated from the inland plains by the Great Barrier Reef. _____
9. The Darling River is the longest river in Australia. _____
10. An ocean is a large body of water. _____

Section 4.

Give answers to the following:

1. Name three seas found in the world.

   _____, _____, _____

2. Name the capital cities of the following countries:

   France _____
   United States _____
   Germany _____
   China _____
   Japan _____
   Italy _____
   Indonesia _____
   New Zealand _____
   Fiji _____
   Papua New Guinea _____

3. On which continent would you find:

   Chile _____
   Zaire _____
   Korea _____
   Tibet _____
   Norway _____
   Canada _____

■ CHAPTER 3

Section 4 continued.

    4. Name the tallest land mountain in the world. _____

    5. Name a wonder of the ancient world. _____

    6. Which is the largest continent? _____

    7. Which continent is also an island? _____

    8. Which scale on a map would show more detail: 1:500 or 1:50 000? _____

Section 5.

    1. There are a number of different environments, such as rainforests, found on the continent of Australia. Name at least two other such environments.

    _____
    _____
    _____

    2. Choose one environment of Australia and briefly describe how humans have, or are, affecting it.

    _____
    _____
    _____

    3. In your opinion, whose responsibility is it to preserve the environments of Australia? Explain your answer. (Continue writing on extra paper if necessary.)

    _____
    _____
    _____
    _____
    _____
    _____
    _____
    _____
    _____
    _____

**EXAMPLE: PRETEST
MATHEMATICS — STAGE 3 (YEARS 5 OR 6)
NUMERACY PRETEST**

Outcome: Student counts, compares and orders whole numbers up to seven digits, and represents them in symbols and words.

1. Write the numeral for:

    twenty-six thousand, two hundred and thirty-seven _____

    four hundred and four thousand, and four _____

    one million, twelve thousand, one hundred and one _____

2. Expand the following numbers:

    35 247 _____

    600 890 _____

3. Write the numeral for:

    2 000 more than 83 264 _____

    10 000 less than 908 835 _____

4. Rewrite in ascending order:

    33 670, 33 076, 33 706, 33 067, 33 760

    _____, _____, _____, _____, _____

5. Make the smallest possible number from 5, 2, 1, 6, 8 _____

6. Make the largest possible number from 9, 0, 6, 8, 4, 5 _____

7. What is the place value of the 8 in each of the following numbers?

    48 603   _____

    282 117   _____

    27 538   _____

    824 009   _____

■ CHAPTER 3

**EXAMPLE: PRETEST
INTERDISCIPLINARY UNIT
(SCIENCE AND TECHNOLOGY/HSIE) — STAGE 3 (YEARS 5 OR 6)
'EXTREME ENVIRONMENTS'**

Using the following concept map outline, brainstorm as much information as you can on the topic 'Extreme Environments'.

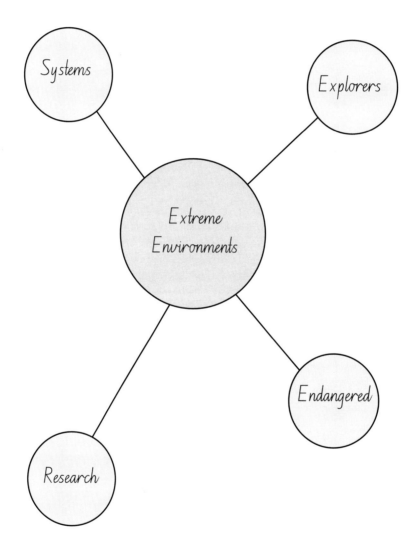

28

CHAPTER 3

Student example of concept map
'Extreme Environments'

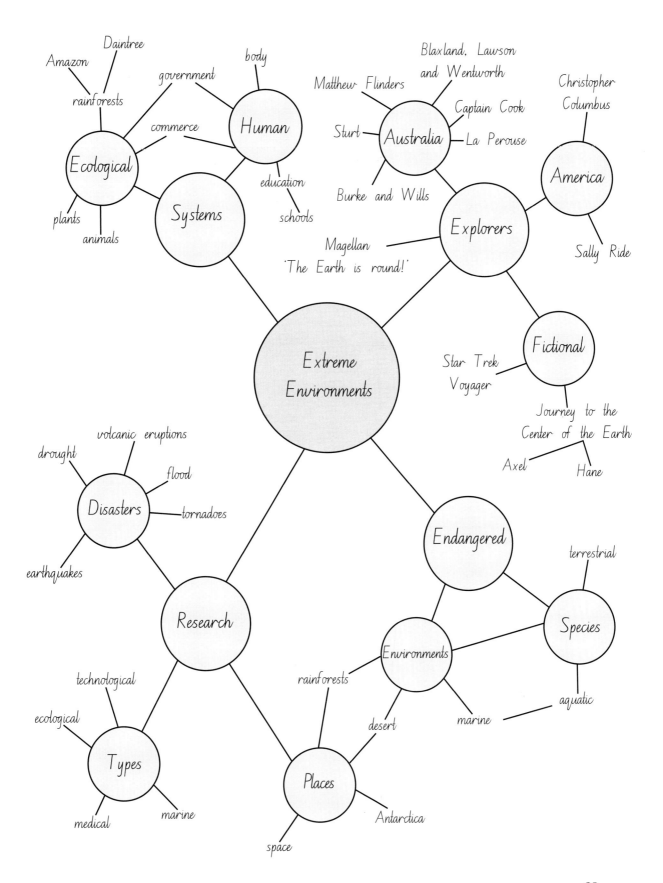

CHAPTER 3

EXAMPLE: PRETEST
ENGLISH — EARLY STAGE 1 (KINDERGARTEN OR YEAR 1)
INFORMAL READING OBSERVATION: RUNNING RECORDS

Today is my birthday. I am 7 years old. I am having a party and my friends are all coming to play. There will be a jumping castle which will be lots of fun. My brother will hide (the) lollies and we will hunt for them. There will be a train cake and ice cream cones for everyone. I am hoping for a remote control car for my present from Grandma and Grandpa. There will be fourteen people and we have already sent out the invitations. Are you coming to my party?

Comments:

Fluent reading. One missed word, one added word.
Stage 1 ceiling – retest using Stage 2 example.

CHAPTER 3

EXAMPLE: PRETEST
ENGLISH — STAGE 2 (YEARS 3 OR 4)
INFORMAL READING OBSERVATION: RUNNING RECORDS

Ben looked out to sea. He combed the waves, looking for the fin that he had come to know so well. His sister, Sarah, was further up the beach, her eyes squinting, searching the waves.

"There it is! About 50m out, Ben, " she shouted, pointing to her right. Ben could not see anything. He stood, riveted [riv-ted], hoping to catch a glimpse. Big swells were appearing behind the breakers and light rain was now falling.

"There it is again!" Sarah shouted. This time he could see two fins. So he has a friend! The rain was falling more heavily now and the two children pulled their jackets over their heads as they ran in the direction of the fins.

A splash of water and there they were – two bottle nosed dolphins – their summer friends. The two children waved goodbye.

"See you next summer," they shouted. The horn of the car tooted and the two children disappeared up the steep ravine [rav-in] to their holiday house for the last time.

Comments:

Fluent, excellent intonation, expression. Two incorrect words.
Stage 2 competency retest using Stage 3 example.

CHAPTER 4
PRINCIPLES OF CURRICULUM DEVELOPMENT

CURRICULUM PRINCIPLES

Once students have been identified as needing some form of differentiation in their learning, the teacher then needs to design learning experiences which will allow these students to achieve their potential. The differentiated curriculum must be academically rigorous and provide intellectual challenge.

Maker (1982) stated that a curriculum which is qualitatively different from the basic or regular curriculum results from the appropriate modification of:

- content,
- process,
- product, and
- learning environment.

These modifications may be provided in three different ways — in breadth and/or depth, in tempo or pace, and in nature or in kind. It is also important that these modifications provide a curriculum that is uniquely appropriate for gifted students rather than being appropriate for all learners (Passow, 1988).

CHAPTER 4

The specific characteristics and needs of gifted students should be taken into account in any curriculum that is designed for them. In all cases, however, gifted students need:
- a climate where they can take risks and make mistakes;
- to work from their strengths;
- an element of choice;
- challenging activities;
- opportunities for creativity and student initiated activities;
- to be encouraged to achieve excellence.

Additionally, the content provided in any curriculum model chosen must be both rigorous and beyond the scope of the regular classroom coverage. *All children benefit from enrichment and all children should benefit from a classroom climate that is accepting and nurturing, and that offers opportunities for creativity and challenge.* However, the needs of gifted students extend beyond these parameters, requiring work that is unusually complex and challenging.

PASSOW'S TEST OF APPROPRIATE CURRICULUM

Perhaps the following three criteria by Passow (1988) best describe how to evaluate the suitability of any curriculum or program for gifted learners:

- *Would* all students want to be involved in such learning experiences?
- *Could* all students participate in such learning experiences?
- *Should* all children be expected to succeed in such learning experiences?

If the answer to these questions is '*yes*', then the curriculum is *not* differentiated for the gifted. *It is important not to confuse what is good whole-school enrichment, with that which is only appropriate for gifted students.* For example, if a guest speaker is invited to a school to talk about motivation and achievement, all students should be given the opportunity to participate and learn from the experience.

A gifted student's true ability will not be apparent if:
- whole-class teaching is used;
- the same lessons and content expectations apply to all;
- the teacher fails to pretest;
- the teacher fails to exempt students if they have already mastered the required skills;
- all students are expected to progress at the same rate;
- tasks and questions are restricted to lower cognitive levels;
- self-esteem issues are not considered.

However, when planning curriculum solely designed for gifted students, the experiences must not be suitable for all students, in either the level and pace of the work, the abstractness and complexity of the content, or the skills to be developed. In this way a program for gifted students is defensible and appropriate.

The following activities are an example of how differentiated learning experiences may be designed to achieve quality learning for gifted students within a mixed-ability, Year 5 classroom in the subject area of Human Society and Its Environment (NSW Board of Studies K–6 Key Learning Area).

EXAMPLE: CURRICULUM DEVELOPMENT
HSIE — STAGE 3 (YEARS 5 OR 6)
'GOLD!'

Task for whole class

1. Choose one of the following topics to research. Present your findings in a creative way. Be prepared to answer questions from a panel of your peers regarding your topic.
   Peter Lalor; Edward Hargraves; Ballarat Reform League; Eureka Stockade; Hill End; Sofala; Kalgoorlie; gold licences; troopers; alluvial gold; reef gold; gold mining equipment; life on the goldfields; Australia after the gold rush.
2. Choose one of the following tasks to complete:
   - List the ingredients and include cooking instructions for a typical meal which would be cooked by a miner on the goldfields.
   - Use modelling clay to make a piece of equipment which a miner might use in the search for gold. Make sure you label your model.
   - Create a diorama depicting one of the well-known goldfields of Australia in the 1850s.

Task for identified gifted students

Complete task 1. from the tasks for the whole class, then choose one of the following tasks to complete:
- Paint a landscape, in a medium of your choice, of a scene from the goldfields. (You may like to look at works by Donald Friend; Jeffrey Smart; Brett Whiteley; Russell Drysdale and others to provide inspiration.)
- Imagine you are a miner travelling to Hill End and you are accompanied by a companion. Write a profile for your companion and include his or her name; age; nationality; family background; occupation; the reason for coming to the goldfields; character traits; annoying habits. Paint or draw a picture of your companion. Make sure his or her clothing is authentic and that you provide an authentic setting.
- Straight from the horse's mouth! Write a short account of a day's journey through rugged bushland from the horse's point of view. In what ways would this account differ from the viewpoint of the horse's 'master'? Explain your opinion.

CHAPTER 4

- Read either *Jeremy Jeremiah* by A. Barron or *A Banner Bold: The Diary of Rosa Aaras, Ballarat Goldfields, 1854* by Nadia Wheatley. Develop a play script for one of the major scenes in the book and perform it for an audience. Include appropriate costuming, props, background materials and music or sound effects in the performance.
- If you were to travel back in time to spend a week on the goldfields, which three modern amenities would you miss most, and why? Which three aspects of modern life would you be happiest to 'escape' from, and why?

The following tables show some of the curriculum models designed for use with gifted students. This book will expand on a number of these and show how they can be used as a helpful framework on which teachers can build appropriate units of work.

CHAPTER 4

**TABLE 2
MODELS FOR CURRICULUM
AND INSTRUCTIONAL DEVELOPMENT**

MODEL	ITS FOCUS	BEST USE
Betts 'Autonomous Learner Model'	Personal development through self-discovery, physical challenge, seminars, independent learning.	Schoolwide Autonomous Learner Model program of courses.
Bloom 'Cognitive Taxonomy Model'	Skills development through content-based experiences.	Schoolwide enrichment. Discussion. Short or long activities.
Bruner 'Structure of the Discipline Model'	Teaching major concepts of a knowledge base through guided discovery, spiralling of concept experiences.	Course development. Activity sequencing. Hands-on experiences.
Clark 'Integrative Curriculum Model'	Simultaneous development of cognitive, affective, intuitive, sociological, and physical strengths.	Discussion. Short or long activities.
Feldhusen 'Purdue Three-Stage Model'	Content enrichment, creative skills development, independent study.	Schoolwide enrichment course development. Short or long activities. Independent study.
Gallagher 'Differentiated Curriculum Model'	Modifying content through novelty, sophistication, enrichment or acceleration.	Schoolwide enrichment course development. Short or long activities.
Jacobs 'Interdisciplinary Model'	Teaching major concepts through integration across disciplines.	Course development. Activity sequencing. Short or long activities.
Kaplan 'Content–Process–Product Grid Model'	Incorporating multiple process skills with differentiated content and non-traditional products.	Project development. Independent study. Long activities.
Kohlberg 'Moral Reasoning Stages Model'	Improving reasoning through confrontation with moral dilemmas, real life or literature based.	Discussion. Short activities.
Maker 'Curriculum Modifications Model'	Modification strategies for content, process, product, and learning environment.	Schoolwide enrichment. Discussion. Independent study. Short or long activities.
Meeker 'Structure of the Intellect Model'	Remediating student weaknesses through individual strengths based on test profile of performance.	Individualised learning. Independent study. Career planning.

37

■ CHAPTER 4

**TABLE 2 CONTINUED
MODELS FOR CURRICULUM
AND INSTRUCTIONAL DEVELOPMENT**

MODEL	ITS FOCUS	BEST USE
Parnes 'Creative Problem Solving Model'	Skill development in divergent problem-solving.	Discussion. Long activities. Competition.
Renzulli and Reis 'Schoolwide Enrichment Model'	Content enrichment, skills development, independent project development with Type 1, 2, and 3 experiences.	Schoolwide enrichment course development. Independent study. Short or long activities.
Stanley and Benbow 'Study of Mathematically Precocious Youth (SMPY) Model'	Content acceleration, especially in mathematics and science.	Course development. Individualised.
Taba 'Teaching Strategies Model'	Inquiry technique for development of generalisations, conflict resolution.	Discussion. Short or long activities.
Tannenbaum 'Enrichment Matrix Model'	Enrichment of total curriculum through telescoping, skill expansion, program augmentation, provisions augmentation, higher-order thinking skills, social/affective remediation.	Individualised learning. Course development. Short or long activities.
Taylor 'Multiple Talents Model' (also Schlichter)	Skill development, remediation in six areas: decision-making, convergent/divergent problem-solving, forecasting, planning, communicating.	Schoolwide enrichment. Discussion. Short or long activities.
Treffinger 'Self-directed Learning Model'	Articulated program for improving skills to do independent study.	Schoolwide enrichment. Independent study. Research activities.
VanTassel-Baska 'Comprehensive Curriculum Model'	Development of major themes through integration across disciplines using morphological key as structure.	Discussion. Short or long activities. Course development.
Williams 'Cognitive–Affective Interaction Model'	Strengthening of students' cognitive and affective creative processes in content-based experiences.	Schoolwide enrichment. Discussion. Short or long activities.

(Rogers, 1996–97)

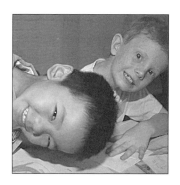

CHAPTER 5
MODELS OF CURRICULUM DEVELOPMENT
MAKER

THE MAKER MODEL OF CURRICULUM DEVELOPMENT FOR GIFTED STUDENTS

ith such a broad array of curriculum models from which to choose, it is sometimes difficult to recognise the most appropriate model for the subject we are teaching, or for the outcomes desired. However, the use of a variety of different models over a period of time is necessary to avoid repetitious presentation of the same model and its own particular style of activities. Different models are appropriate for different students at different times and not all curriculum strategies are suitable for each student.

Many of the models incorporate strategies for the modification of content, process, product and learning environment as proposed by Maker (1982), using a variety of techniques, and a combination of these techniques may be appropriate in many cases.

The primary purpose of curriculum development for gifted students is to provide experiences for these students that are qualitatively different from those provided for all children. Maker (1982) described qualitatively different programs as those which are designed to:

- enhance or recognise what is different or special about the students for whom they were designed;
- provide concepts at higher levels of abstraction or greater complexity; emphasise the development of higher order thinking skills; and
- enable all students to realise their full potential.

In order to differentiate curriculum for gifted students, we need to modify the four primary areas of curriculum development:
- content;
- process;
- product; and
- learning environment.

Content

The content of the curriculum comprises the ideas, concepts and information presented to students. To make this content more appropriate for gifted students, it must be made more complex, more abstract, more varied and organised differently (Maker, 1982). For example, in a unit of work for Year 6 on 'Courage and Survival', a core content outcome for all students is:

> Students will understand, and be able to give examples of, situations or events where people or characters have shown courage in order to survive.

The associated outcome for gifted students could be:

> Students will understand and be able to give examples of courage and survival, exploring the relationships between courage and the 'will to live', and between faith and adversity.

Process

The process or methodology is the way in which the content is presented to students, and this includes the type of questions asked of them and the mental and physical activities expected of them. For the process to be more appropriate for gifted students, the teacher may modify the level of thinking required, the pace of teaching and the type of approach used. For example, in the same unit on 'Courage and Survival', a core activity could be written as:

> Students will read fiction and nonfiction centring on the theme of courage and survival. Activities may be based on texts such as: *Island of the Blue Dolphins* (O'Dell), and *Anne Frank: The Diary of a Young Girl* (Frank).

The activity for gifted students could written as:

> Students will read fiction and nonfiction centring on the theme of courage and survival. Activities may include comparisons of novels such as: *Number the Stars* (Lowry), *Earthsong* (Kelleher), *Tomorrow When the War Began* (Marsden), and *Roll of Thunder, Hear My Cry* (Taylor), with nonfiction selections such as: *Escape from Sarajevo* (Mattingley), *The Endless Steppe* (Hautzig), and *I Can Jump Puddles* (Marshall).

Product

The nature of products expected from gifted students may also be modified to be more appropriate. Products may entail a multitude of formats, all of which require the information or content to be directed towards a specific audience, and to be evaluated by someone other than the developer.

It is important that these products address a real problem or concern rather than be simply summations of content. Equally, the presentation of these products should be to a 'real' audience, able to professionally evaluate the work. As with content and process, the importance of developing higher-order thinking skills is paramount in the presentation of any product.

The following examples of products from the unit on 'Courage and Survival' would be the result of the activities mentioned in the previous section on process.

Core product:
Compare one of the fictional 'courage and survival' novels with one nonfictional account, describing the similarities and differences between the two styles.

Gifted students' product:
Compare one of the fictional 'courage and survival' novels with one nonfictional account, describing the similarities and differences between the two styles. How does the development of the protagonist in the fictional work compare to that of the main 'voice' in the nonfictional work? In which style of writing, fiction or nonfiction, does the theme of courage and survival have the greater impact? Give reasons for your opinion.

Learning environment

In order to successfully implement modifications to the content, process and product, it is important to make changes to the learning environment. Maker (1982) described the learning environment for gifted students as needing to:
- be student-centred rather than teacher-centred;
- encourage independence rather than dependence;
- be open rather than closed;
- be accepting instead of judgemental;
- be complex and abstract rather than simple and concrete;
- permit and encourage high mobility instead of low mobility.

Changes to the learning environment may be achieved, for example, in a mixed-ability classroom by allowing those students who have proven mastery in the core curriculum to work on independent projects. This would require them to work on a complex topic both within the classroom and outside it.

The tables on the following pages link the appropriate strategies for the modification of content, process, product and learning environment with correlating models, definitions and methods. For example, if a teacher wants to modify the regular curriculum with regards to the complexity of the content, activities in the models developed by Maker (1982), Gallagher (1975), Tannenbaum (1986), Kaplan (1974), Bloom (1956), Taba (1964) and Kohlberg (1971) can be used.

CHAPTER 5

TABLE 3
STRATEGIES FOR MODIFYING THE CONTENT FOR GIFTED LEARNERS
THE MAKER MODEL

STRATEGY	DEFINITION	HOW	DEVELOPER
Abstraction	Going beyond the facts, examining underlying ideas, symbolism, meanings of the content.	Inquiry Projects Papers Independent study	Maker (Taba) (Bruner) (Kaplan)
Complexity	Posing challenging questions or situations that force the learner to deal with content intricacies; greater breadth or depth.	Inquiry Projects Independent study Activities	Maker (Gallagher) (Tannenbaum) (Kaplan, Bloom) (Taba, Kohlberg)
Variety	Sampling different types of related content, often from other disciplines or subject areas. Exposure to new ideas or content.	Inquiry Projects Independent study Activities	Maker (Jacobs) (VanTassel-Baska) (Kaplan)
Organisation	Selecting new arrangements of content, e.g. functional similarities, categorical groups, descriptive similarities, whole–part ideas.	Group work Inquiry Projects Activities	Maker (Bruner) (Clark, Betts) (Gallagher) (Stanley)
Study of people	Relating content to people, the human situation and human problems.	Projects Independent study Papers Group work	Maker (Bruner) (Kohlberg) (Parnes, Betts)
Methods of inquiry	Relating content to the methods and procedures used by people in a field or subject area.	Independent study Group work Projects Activities	Maker (Bruner) (Renzulli) (Williams, Taylor)
Telescoping, tempo, pacing, subject skipping, compacting, testing out	Shortening the amount of time required for completion of work and by-passing mastered content.	Independent study Group work Individual Educational Programs (IEPs)	Tannenbaum (Gallagher) (Stanley) (Renzulli)
Higher-order thinking skills (HOTS), analysis, synthesis, evaluation	Utilising higher-level thinking skills for regular content processing.	Inquiry Projects Papers Independent study Group work	Bloom, Maker (Tannenbaum) (Taba, Kaplan) (Kohlberg, Renzulli) (Meeker, Williams)

STRATEGY	DEFINITION	HOW	DEVELOPER
Open-ended, paradox, analogy, intuitive expression, tolerance of ambiguity	Utilising divergent thinking skills for regular content processing.	Inquiry Group work Projects Essays	Williams, Maker (Renzulli) (Taylor, Parnes) (Kaplan, Clark) (Meeker)
Discovery	Requiring students to progress through a series of steps of inquiry to draw own conclusions, answers and generalisations.	Inquiry Projects Independent study	Bruner, Maker (Betts, Clark) (Parnes, Renzulli) (Treffinger, Taba) (Gallagher, Williams)
Proof and reasoning	Students required to cite sources; clues given; logic used in drawing conclusions.	Inquiry Independent study Projects	Maker, Great Books (Bruner, Bloom) (Taylor, Williams) (Tannenbaum, Taba)
Freedom of choice	Providing opportunities for self-directed, independent study.	Projects Independent study Papers	Maker (Treffinger)
Group interactions, simulations	Posing of structured, simulated situations for group problem-solving.	Independent study Projects Group work	Maker (Parnes, Taba) (Kohlberg, Betts) (Williams, Taylor)
Real problems	Learners investigate the kinds of questions and problems investigated by professionals; 'real-life' problems.	Inquiry Projects Independent study Group work	Maker (Renzulli, Bruner) (Parnes, Taylor) (Kohlberg, Betts) (Treffinger, Kaplan)
Real audiences	Student products are developed for the expected evaluation by professionals or experts in that field or discipline.	Inquiry Group work Projects Papers	Maker (Renzulli, Bruner) (Taylor, Parnes)
Evaluation	Teacher assessment using pre-established criteria combined with student self-evaluation.	Group work Projects Independent study	Maker (Renzulli, Bruner) (Parnes, Taylor)
Transformations, visualisations	Students are encouraged to suggest practical uses for what has been learned, rather than simply producing summarisations; uses may be in non-traditional media.	Papers Independent study Projects Group work Activities	Maker, Williams (Renzulli, Kaplan) (Bruner, Betts) (Gallagher, Taylor)

■ CHAPTER 5

TABLE 3 CONTINUED
STRATEGIES FOR MODIFYING THE CONTENT FOR GIFTED LEARNERS
THE MAKER MODEL

STRATEGY	DEFINITION	HOW	DEVELOPER
Student-centered	Learning experiences based on student talents or interests.	Discussion Projects Group work	Maker (Betts, Bruner)
Independence, encouragement	Tolerance for student initiative.	Independent study Projects Activities	Maker, Clark (Treffinger) (Parnes)
Openness	Tolerance for many ideas; removing of restrictions on learning environments.	Activities Projects Independent study Inquiry	Maker, Clark (Williams) (Parnes, Taylor)
Accepting	Suspension of judgement about ideas; tolerance for divergence; focus on understanding ideas.	Inquiry Activities Projects	Maker, Clark
Complexity in learning setting	Stimulating physical setting; complex intellectual tasks; variety of materials; support.	Activities Inquiry Projects	Maker, Clark
High mobility	Flexible movement in and out of classrooms.	Activities Projects Independent study Inquiry	Maker, Clark
Divergence, fluency, flexibility, elaboration, originality, risk-taking, curiosity, complexity, imagination	Encouragement of divergent thinking and behaviour. Generation of multiple ideas; different directions, details and improvements; uniqueness; taking chances; exploring; liking challenge; using visual images inside mind.	Activities Projects Inquiry Discussion Independent study	Williams (Meeker, Taylor)

(Rogers, 1996–97)

Some examples of Maker model curriculum modifications

The following subject-specific modification examples incorporate ideas that may be used as class, group or individual activities. Each example may be used separately as an in-lesson activity for identified gifted students or as part of a differentiated unit of work for a mixed-ability class.

EXAMPLE: MAKER MODIFICATIONS
SCIENCE AND TECHNOLOGY — STAGE 1 (YEARS 1 OR 2)
TRANSPORT

Content modifications

Abstraction
What do you think a future invention for transport may be?

Organisation
Conduct a traffic survey from your school gate for at least ten minutes. Focus on a specific area, such as: types of vehicles; number of vehicles passing in ten minutes; number of passengers in each vehicle. Use a table to organise your results.

Variety
Listen to the sounds of traffic. Create a piece of music which may soothe and relax a stressed bus driver.

Study of people
Investigate the people who improved the effectiveness of air travel. Present your findings in a creative way.

Methods of inquiry
Use the Internet to find out how many different ways you can travel from London to Sydney. Use a world map to show different routes and methods of transport. Which would you choose? Explain why.

Process modifications

Higher-order thinking skills

Analysis
Survey the children in the class and discover how their parents travel to work. Record and present your findings. Why do you think these results occurred?

Synthesis
Create an advertising jingle to encourage people to walk more, rather than using 'wheels'.

Evaluation
Study your local transport facilities. Decide which is the best method of transport to school and justify your choice.

Open-ended processing

Analogy
How is a train like a caterpillar? How is transport like the Internet?

Tolerance for ambiguity
What would happen if planes were suddenly banned? Write an explanation of your ideas.

Intuitive expression
Write an onomatopoeic poem based on the sounds of transport.

Discovery
Discover how a hovercraft works. Draw a diagram or build a model.

Freedom of choice
Choose any method of public transport and design an advertisement to attract the general public to use it more often.

Product modifications

Real world problems
Write a letter to your local newspaper related to a local transport issue.

EXAMPLE: MAKER MODIFICATIONS
HSIE/SOSE — STAGE 3 (YEAR 6)
'CULTURES OF THE WORLD'

Content modifications

Abstraction
What is meant by the term 'cultural diversity'?

Complexity
Choose a definition for the word 'culture' and then use this to distinguish one culture from another.

Variety
Collect and study examples of music, art and costume or dress from two different cultures. How do these examples affect our understanding of these cultures?

Study of people
Choose a famous person from each of two separate cultural groups. Compare their lives, discussing how their cultural backgrounds affected their development and success.

Methods of inquiry
What is a sociologist? Give examples of at least two well-known sociologists, discussing their work in comparison to that of an historian.

Process modifications

Higher-order thinking skills

Analysis
Many cultures have wise sayings which have been 'handed down' over generations. How true are these? How similar are they from one culture to another?

Synthesis
Read some folk tales from two different cultural groups. Create a new folk tale in the style of each cultural group describing a natural phenomenon.

Evaluation
Should all schools have a day to celebrate cultural diversity? Give reasons for your opinion.

Open-ended processing

Paradox
Can a culture disappear?

Analogy
How is a culture like a mosaic?

Tolerance for ambiguity
What if cross-cultural friendships were discouraged in Australia?

Intuitive expression
Imagine you have to live in a different cultural context to your current one. How would your life be different? How would you feel?

Discovery
Keep a journal for a week of all the different cultures with which you come into contact. Decide which one of these cultures has the greatest impact on your life and explain why.

Freedom of choice
Study a specific culture of your choice. What makes this culture so unique?

CHAPTER 5

Product modifications

Real world problems
Issues of 'cultural diversity' often bring with them conflict and resistance to change. Choose a present-day example of such a conflict and examine some of the responses to the problems that have been, or are being, tried. Suggest some further ways to bring about a solution to this situation.

Real audiences
Enlist feedback on some of the solutions you have devised from a leader or representative of the culture or cultures involved.

Transformations
Create a cultural tapestry for one of the cultures you have examined, which would include historical, traditional and social representations.

USING A MAKER MODIFICATIONS MATRIX

When creating appropriate activities or units of work for gifted students, it is important to ensure that there is a balance between content and process modifications. By utilising a matrix system to devise activities, it is easier to see at a glance whether balance is being achieved.

The following matrices are further examples of Maker modifications in the areas of content and process. Where possible, both subject and topic are nominated for each matrix, and a blank matrix is supplied in the appendix to assist you in creating your own examples.

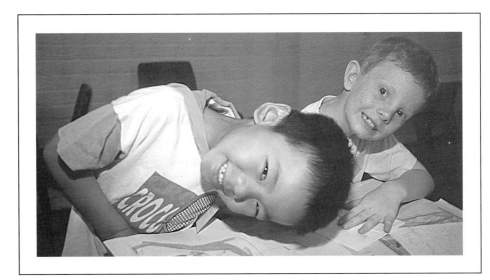

47

TABLE 4
MAKER MODIFICATIONS MATRIX
ENGLISH — STAGE 3 (YEAR 5)
***BLUEBACK* BY TIM WINTON**

CONTENT / PROCESS	STUDY OF PEOPLE	VARIETY	ABSTRACTION
ANALYSIS	At the end of high school, Abel went away to 'study the sea' at university. What does a marine biologist do that differs from what an 'ichthyologist' does?	What are some of the courses available at universities to 'study the sea'? Compare some of the different careers you can pursue if you want to work with the sea.	What did Abel's mother mean by 'The ocean is sick'?
PARADOX	As an adult, Abel comes to realise that his mother is the one who understands the sea although she had not studied about it at university like he had. Why is this an important realisation for him?	There are many places in the world where creatures have learned to live and cooperate with humans. What are some examples of this? What are some of the dangers involved in this type of relationship?	During the summer of Abel's thirteenth year, he learned that 'there was nothing in nature as cruel and savage as a greedy human being'. Why then do people often describe the sea as 'cruel and savage'?
PROOF AND REASONING	After the cyclone hit the bay, Dora decided to 'help the bay live'. How did she do this? What sort of information do authorities need to decide to make an area a wildlife sanctuary?	Blueback lived in the bay throughout Abel's life. There are a number of creatures in the world which enjoy lifespans as long as this and some, much longer. Investigate some of these, discovering how scientists have proved these creatures' longevity.	Dora told her son: 'We come from water…We belong to it…' What did she mean? Prove that her statement is correct.

From Gross, MacLeod, Drummond and Merrick (2001) *Gifted Students in Primary Schools: Differentiating the Curriculum* Sydney: GERRIC.

TABLE 5
MAKER MODIFICATIONS MATRIX
CREATIVE AND VISUAL ARTS — STAGE 2 (YEARS 3 OR 4)
'REAL AND IMAGINED CREATURES'

CONTENT / PROCESS	INTUITIVE EXPRESSION	VARIETY	ABSTRACTION
ANALYSIS	Pretend you are an insect visiting your classroom. Create a comic strip comparing two humorous incidents which occurred while you were there.	Collect a variety of pictures illustrating insect wings. How do they compare to artists' impressions of fairy wings?	Studying artworks: How are the monsters in *Where the Wild Things Are* similar to and different from the dragon in Graeme Base's *The Discovery of Dragons*?
COMPLEXITY	Listen to Rimsky-Korsakov's *The Flight of the Bumble Bee*. Imagine you are a bumblebee. Depict your travels during one day using a variety of media.	Research butterflies or dragonflies. Choose one species of dragonfly and using graphic pencils or watercolours, sketch your favourite.	Using a computer drawing program, create a detailed artwork depicting the way a wild animal, or your pet, would see you through their eyes.
DISCOVERY	Invent a newly discovered insect. Produce a detailed anatomical drawing of your new insect.	New insects are being classified every year. Make a collage of some recent classifications.	Are there fairies at the bottom of the garden? Design a three-dimensional wire and plaster bandage model of a dragon or insect which may look like a fairy at the bottom of your garden.

From Gross, MacLeod, Drummond and Merrick (2001) *Gifted Students in Primary Schools: Differentiating the Curriculum* Sydney: GERRIC.

TABLE 6
MAKER MODIFICATIONS MATRIX
PD, H & PE* – STAGE 1 (YEARS 1 OR 2)
'POSITIVE HEALTH CHOICES'

CONTENT / PROCESS	STUDY OF PEOPLE	VARIETY	COMPLEXITY
ANALYSIS	Interview your dentist and your doctor to discover what a typical day may be like for them. Discover why they think people might avoid visiting them. How were their days and opinions similar and different?	How many different types of doctors are there? Make a list to compare what each type does.	Where are first-aid supplies stored in your school? Are they being stored safely? Can this be improved?
PARADOX	There is a saying: 'An apple a day keeps the doctor away'. Where did this saying come from? Can the same be true for a dentist?	Collect a variety of sayings about our health. How many of these are true? Explain.	'School canteens should only sell healthy foods.' Investigate the pros and cons of this statement.
EVALUATION	Who discovered penicillin? Why was the discovery so important?	Survey the class on whether they enjoy visiting the dentist. Why? Why not?	Should teachers have to wear hats when they are on playground duty? Give three reasons for and three reasons against the idea.

From Gross, MacLeod, Drummond and Merrick (2001) *Gifted Students in Primary Schools: Differentiating the Curriculum* Sydney: GERRIC
* Personal Development, Health and Physical Education

CHAPTER 6
MODELS OF CURRICULUM DEVELOPMENT
BLOOM/KRATHWOHL

BLOOM'S AND KRATHWOHL'S COGNITIVE AND AFFECTIVE TAXONOMIES

The development of higher-order thinking skills in students through the curriculum was an important factor in the work of Bloom (1956) and Krathwohl, Bloom and Masia (1964). These authors designed taxonomies based on cognitive and affective behaviours that are applicable to any subject area and any level of instruction. The main principle in the process is to provide a simple structure for developing learning activities in order to take students through a sequential developmental process (Maker, 1982).

The major premise of these taxonomies is that they are hierarchical, with each level depending on all the levels below it. For example, to be able to operate at the application level of thinking, the processes of knowledge and comprehension must also be operational. Although Bloom, Krathwohl and Masia intended the taxonomies to be applicable to all students, gifted students, whilst still needing to show the ability to work at the lower levels, should spend more time working at the higher, more complex and abstract levels.

The cognitive taxonomy consists of six levels:

1. knowledge
2. comprehension
3. application
4. analysis
5. synthesis
6. evaluation

The affective taxonomy consists of five levels:

1. receiving or attending
2. responding
3. valuing
4. organisation
5. characterisation by a value complex

Whilst the cognitive taxonomy is the one more commonly used by teachers when developing activities or units of work, the two taxonomies are intertwined and often the attainment of one level in the cognitive domain is dependent on a correlating attainment in the affective domain. For example, in order to develop values, as in value complex, the ability to evaluate choices is also necessary.

BLOOM'S TAXONOMY

The following description of Bloom's taxonomy, with suggestions for curriculum implementation, has been developed by Rogers (1996–1997).

Level 1: Knowledge — remember or recall. This level requires the mastery of facts, including terminologies, conventions, trends and sequences, classifications, categories, criteria, methodologies, principles, generalisations, theories and structures.

1. Specifics   (Trivial Pursuit answer)
2. Terms   (What is giftedness?)
3. Facts   (Molecular formula for water: H_2O)
4. Conventions   (Grammar)
5. Trends   ('Baby boomers' generation)
6. Classifications   (The animal kingdom)
7. Criteria   (What constitutes good nutrition?)
8. Methods   (Scientific method of investigation)
9. Universals   (What makes a culture?)
10. Theories   (Newton's third law)

Level 2: Comprehension involves the ability to show understanding of concepts by restating them by translation (paraphrasing or restating ideas), interpretation (explaining or summarising ideas), and extrapolation (extension of trends). Students demonstrate understanding by:

1. translation — restating knowledge from:
    A. one level of abstraction to another (own words);
    B. one symbolic form to another (musical score);
    C. one verbal form to another (prose to poetry);

2. interpretation — demonstrating knowledge by:
   A. generalising: finding surface commonalities;
   B. clarifying: restating to make clearer;
   C. distinguishing between parts: itemising elements that make up the whole;
   D. qualifying: setting limitations on the whole;
3. extrapolation — using knowledge to predict next steps.

Level 3: Application. This level moves beyond that of comprehension in that students are required to apply previously encountered rules or concepts to new situations, rather than simply demonstrating their understanding in a known situation. Students transfer understanding to other concrete, real-life and hypothetical situations, providing examples to illustrate their understanding.

Level 4: Analysis. At this level, students are required to break down learned knowledge to be able to recognise, identify, distinguish and infer assumptions, opinions, motives, bias and frameworks. This is identified by their ability to:

1. recognise unstated assumptions;
2. distinguish fact from opinion;
3. identify underlying motives;
4. comprehend interrelationships;
5. check for consistency and inconsistency;
6. relate cause and effect;
7. distinguish relevant and irrelevant details or arguments;
8. recognise logical fallacies;
9. distinguish relative importance of details;
10. identify underlying organisation, framework of major ideas;
11. infer points of view;
12. recognise bias;
13. identify tone and mood;
14. identify underlying problems;
15. recognise purpose;
16. identify personal importance or use.

Level 5: Synthesis. At the synthesis level, students are able to produce unique products by combining elements of understanding. This combination may produce:

1. a unique communication;
2. a plan;
3. a set of abstract relationships, e.g. a theory of taxonomy.

Level 6: Evaluation involves the ability to make judgements, choices or decisions based on a set of predetermined standards or criteria. This evaluation is based on:

1. internal evidence: personally developed set of standards or set developed specifically for given knowledge domain;
2. external criteria: aesthetics, harmony, etc.

The following chart suggests appropriate words to use when framing questions and/or activities in Bloom's units of work:

Knowledge questions:

What	Distinguish	Recall	Write
When	Identify	Reorganise	Who
Which	List	Indicate	Show
Define	Name	State	Tell
Describe	Where	How	

Comprehension questions:

Compare	Distinguish	Inform	What
Demonstrate	Explain	Fill in	Infer
Reorder	Rephrase	Relate	Show
Rearrange	Extend	Give example	Draw
Predict	Estimate	Translate	Describe

Application questions:

Apply	Demonstrate	Construct	Test
Develop	Plan	Solve	Build
Indicate	Choose	Show work	Check
Consider	Try	How would	Tell
Transfer	Redo	Give example	Use

Analysis questions:

Analyse	Discriminate	Relate	Identify
Categorise	Distinguish	Explain	Split
Describe how	Recognise	Assume	Why
Classify	Support	What factors	Compare
Indicate	What do you	Contrast	

Synthesis questions:

Write	Suggest	Plan	Imagine
Think of a way	How	Solve	Create
Originate	Develop	Synthesise	Derive
Propose	Make up	Construct	Suggest
Put together	Conclude	Produce	

Evaluation questions:

Choose	Judge	Consider	Defend
What is	Check	Evaluate	Indicate
Select	Propose	Test	Support
Conclude	Argue	Debate	Side
Categorise	Most appropriate	Weigh	

CHAPTER 6

KRATHWOHL'S TAXONOMY

The following description discusses Krathwohl's taxonomy.

Level 1: Receiving — listening or attending to classroom activities. This level requires the ability to listen attentively and awareness of the surrounding environment. For example, this may be demonstrated when an activity involves students listening to a musical or dramatic recording in a classroom without being distracted.

Level 2: Responding — actively participating in tasks or activities. For example, a student may share personal reflections in a class discussion, volunteer for a task or help a peer.

Level 3: Valuing. This level moves beyond that of receiving or responding in that students are required to demonstrate their commitment or involvement to particular processes, people or behaviours. This may be shown through a student's concern for the welfare of others or in their attitude towards solving problems.

Level 4: Organising. At this level, students are required to bring together different values to enable conflict resolution and the construction of value-system frameworks. Students may demonstrate this by accepting responsibility for their own behaviour, by understanding their individual strengths and weaknesses, or by valuing the importance of their own, and others, opinions.

Level 5: Characterisation by value. At this level, students are not only able to define their own beliefs and values, but will act in accordance with that value system. For example, a student at this level may show self-discipline, independent working behaviours and have a plan developed for their own future studies.

The following chart suggests appropriate verbs to use when framing questions and/or activities in Krathwohl's units of work:

Receiving questions:

Ask	Distinguish	Recall	Select
Choose	Identify	Recognise	Reply
Describe	Listen	Observe	Use
Differentiate	Name	Accept	Feel
Hold	Locate	Follow	Perceive

Responding questions:

Answer	Help	Write	Label
Assist	Perform	Tell	Practice
Conform	Present	Applaud	Cooperate
Greet	Read	Approve	Contribute
Discuss	Recite	Command	Satisfy

Valuing questions:

Complete	Invite	Report	Explain
Describe	Join	Share	Relinquish
Follow	Justify	Study	Debate
Form	Propose	Work	Believe
Initiate	Read	Argue	Persuade

Organising questions:

Adhere	Define	Prepare	Generalise
Alter	Explain	Relate	Integrate
Arrange	Identify	Synthesise	Organise
Combine	Modify	Balance	Formulate
Compare	Order	Defend	Articulate

Characterisation by values questions:

Act	Question	Propose	Develop
Discriminate	Solve	Review	Change
Display	Use	Judge	Conclude
Influence	Verify	Manage	Rate
Qualify	Listen	Resolve	Resist

Here are some practical examples of how the Bloom and Krathwohl taxonomies can assist us in developing units in specific subject areas. They have been developed in a matrix highlighting the content, the higher-order thinking skills and the product involved. The areas of knowledge and comprehension are important and many teachers feel confident with their skills in creating activities and tasks in those areas. However, teachers may require greater assistance in activities and tasks for the higher-order thinking skills and so we have concentrated on these skills only. A blank matrix is also provided in the Appendix on which to develop your own examples.

CHAPTER 6

**TABLE 7
BLOOM ENRICHMENT MATRIX
ENGLISH — EARLY STAGE 1 (KINDERGARTEN)**
WHERE THE WILD THINGS ARE **BY MAURICE SENDAK**

CONTENT	APPLICATION	ANALYSIS	SYNTHESIS	EVALUATION
Characterisation	Create a new monster for an Australian version of this book.	Why are the monsters called 'wild things'? What other names could the author use for these monsters?	Write a story pretending you are Max. Make a new name for yourself. Travel to your imaginary land using a different type of transport.	Would you like to be Max? Why or why not?
Use of language in the story	Choose three words in the book that are new to you. Find out what they mean and explain them in your own words. (**Note.** If there are no words that are new to a student, then ask them to see if they can substitute three new words to improve words already in the story.)	What words could you use other than 'terrible' to describe the monsters?	Construct a *Where the Wild Things Are* illustrated dictionary for the words you find in the text.	Select your three favourite descriptive words from the story. Why are they your favourites? Are there any words you would change? What words would you use instead?
Illustration	Try Maurice Sendak's style of illustrating. Draw an imaginary monster of your own in the same style.	Look at the artwork in the book. What do you notice about the use of white space and text as the book progresses? Why does the author do this? Discuss your ideas with a small group of classmates.	Create a series of illustrations for your own imaginary land using only two colours.	Do you like the illustrations in this book? Explain why.
Plot	Tell the story of *Where the Wild Things Are* on to a tape for preschool children to listen to as they look at the book.	Explain how Max could see and hear so much in such a short time.	What would you need to buy for a party like the 'wild rumpus'?	If you were the author, how would you change the story?
Theme	Construct a vehicle which Max might travel on in his next adventure.	Why is Max's supper still warm when he returns home?	Write Max's next adventure.	What is imagination? When is imagination important? Write a story to show a time when you have used your imagination.

From Gross, MacLeod, Drummond and Merrick (2001) *Gifted Students in Primary Schools: Differentiating the Curriculum* Sydney: GERRIC.

■ CHAPTER 6

**TABLE 8
BLOOM ENRICHMENT MATRIX
SCIENCE — STAGE 1 (YEARS 1 OR 2)
'LIVING THINGS'**

CONTENT	APPLICATION	ANALYSIS	SYNTHESIS	EVALUATION
Animals	Build a suitable environment for a class pet.	Choose an insect and research its body parts. (You may collect an insect and observe it for a short time before releasing it.) Draw what you see in detail, then research and label the various body parts, explaining the importance of each part.	Imagine you are holding a 'pet day' at school. Suggest which animal might win the most unusual pet category and why.	Are computers living things? Write an argument for and against this question.
Life cycles	Create an artwork depicting how living things change according to the seasons. Use collage or another creative art form.	Examine the life cycle of a frog. What would happen to the cycle if the pond were polluted? Write an explanation of your ideas.	Write a poem about 'The Web of Life'.	Choose a small section of the playground. Categorise the plants. Which is the hardiest for the playground environment? Why?
Habitats	Design an enclosure for an animal of your choice for a new zoo. Consider its needs and the requirements for the viewing public.	Choose ten animals. Classify their habitats using two different definitions.	Choose a source of energy, e.g. sun, wind, water. Design an experiment which shows how this source can be used by living things like humans, other animals and plants.	Study the playground environment. How appropriate is it for living things? How could the environment be improved to encourage the presence of more living things?
Human interaction	Choose an animal which visits your school. Write a plan to protect its habitat from human interaction.	How much paper is used in your school every week? Does this seem reasonable? Is paper being wasted? How might paper be conserved and what effect will that have on the environment?	Consider three animals which are now extinct. Why do animals become extinct? How do humans interfere in the life cycle of some animals? Create a web diagram showing how humans may interfere in the life cycle of one animal.	Some animals evoke strong emotions in humans, e.g. fear of snakes or insects. Create a list of animals which evoke a strong human response, describing the type of response generally found. Why do these responses occur? How do people overcome their fear of certain animals like insects?

From Gross, MacLeod, Drummond and Merrick (2001) *Gifted Students in Primary Schools: Differentiating the Curriculum* Sydney: GERRIC.

TABLE 9
BLOOM ENRICHMENT MATRIX
PD, H & PE — STAGE 2 (YEARS 3 OR 4)
'GREAT EXPECTATIONS' *

CONTENT	VALUE	ORGANISE	CHARACTERISE
Personal identity: similarities and differences; strengths; setting relevant goals for addressing change.	In a small group, share the qualities and strengths that you admire in a friend. Create a mind map to summarise the group discussion.	Create a chart in which you identify the things about yourself that you can change and the things over which you have no control.	Propose a plan to bring about positive changes in one area of your life that will enable you to build on your strengths.
The body: senses; heredity.	Describe, reflect, compare and discuss the various influences on your life and your behaviour, e.g. diet, interests, values, family, peers, media.	Identify and define patterns of common traits and behaviours of family members.	Choose a member of your family who appears to share many common characteristics with yourself. Develop a list of these commonalities. Develop a list of the features which make each of you unique and then compare the two lists.
Changes: changing friendships; feelings; needs; environments; coping with change.	Design a personal timeline which indicates significant changes or turning points in your life. Ask a family member to create a mirror timeline for the same years of his or her life. How are these timelines similar and different?	Do you have the same friends now as you did two years ago? Why or why not? How have the patterns of friendship changed in your life? Can you explain why?	Good friends may have higher expectations for you than you have for yourself. Reflect on the extent to which this applies to your friendships.
Values: respecting different values; rights and responsibilities; identity; goals.	Initiate a discussion in a small group about the responsibilities you each have as a friend. Are your expectations of friendship different? Why or why not? Maintain a diary for a week noting the things you do for your friends and the things they do for you.	Identify the common values held by your friends. Would these values be common for all age groups or cultures? Why or why not?	Provide an action plan to be used in your classroom to deal with disputes in friendships. Trial this plan on a hypothetical conflict. You may like to role-play how this conflict may be resolved.

From Gross, MacLeod, Drummond and Merrick (2001) *Gifted Students in Primary Schools: Differentiating the Curriculum* Sydney: GERRIC.
* Activities adapted from core module tasks, found in the NSW Board of Studies Syllabus for PD, H & PE (K-6)

■ CHAPTER 6

TABLE 10
BLOOM ENRICHMENT MATRIX
PD, H & PE — STAGE 2 (YEARS 3 OR 4)
'KNOWING ME, KNOWING YOU' *

CONTENT	VALUE	ORGANISE	CHARACTERISE
Relationships: recognising and accepting differences.	In a small group, share your ideas about the ways in which good friends show that they value the positive qualities in others.	Brainstorm the advantages and disadvantages of being different. Create a class list of how you might positively support and celebrate each other's differences.	In the next few days, choose one of these ideas to show a good friend how much you value their friendship or lend support to a classmate who may feel different.
Peers: acting on concern for others.	Describe a situation when someone in the playground showed concern for someone else. What positive behaviours resulted from this action? Could there have been a different outcome? Why or why not? Explain.	Re-enact the playground situation showing two alternative outcomes, one positive and one negative. At what point can a negative behaviour be changed to positive? Role-play an example of this.	Develop a proposal encouraging your fellow students to support a particular charity; or develop an action plan outlining the steps needed to encourage students in your school to consider the needs of others.
Communication: managing conflict situations and negotiations.	Select and analyse an example of a conflict between two groups of people that you have heard about in the news.	Compare the conflict selected to a similar situation in your own life or in your school. Determine whether the same approach to address the conflict would be appropriate to your situation and why.	Conflicts often arise in the course of group work. Collaborate with a small group of classmates to devise a short list of 'rules for good group work'.
Groups: roles, rights and responsibilities.	Discuss some of the responsibilities students have in caring for and supporting each other at school.	Examine the United Nations Charter on Children's Rights and identify areas where personal rights may sometimes conflict with the needs of the group, and where the ways of achieving personal goals may contribute to the well-being of the group.	Set a goal for developing one of your personal strengths. Propose a timeline to achieve this goal. Collaborate with classmates on a plan to support each member of the class to achieve, and then celebrate the achievement of, a significant personal goal.

From Gross, MacLeod, Drummond and Merrick (2001) *Gifted Students in Primary Schools: Differentiating the Curriculum* Sydney: GERRIC.
* Activities adapted from core module tasks, found in the NSW Board of Studies Syllabus for PD, H & PE (K-6)

CHAPTER 7
MODELS OF CURRICULUM DEVELOPMENT
KAPLAN

KAPLAN'S CONTENT–PROCESS–PRODUCT MODEL

aplan described a differentiated curriculum as 'a set of learning experiences related to a given theme' allowing for 'comprehensive and integrated educational opportunities for gifted students' (Kaplan, 1986, p. 181). The elements of the learning experience surround a central theme to provide extensive and interconnected learning. Kaplan suggests that when attempting to select a central theme it should:

- be related to and/or based on a discipline;
- be significant to study;
- not be age or time-dependent;
- allow for a variety of teacher-directed and student-selected options for study.
  (Kaplan, 1986, p. 185)

As with the Maker model, the Kaplan model examines the differentiation of curriculum in the areas of content, process, product and learning environment.

Content

When selecting content for the curriculum, Kaplan lists the following rules:
- The specific selection of content should be referenced to the organising element or theme.
- The topic areas to be studied within the theme should be multidisciplinary.
- The topics selected for the theme should represent those that are expected for all students to learn.
- The topics selected should allow for the integration of subject areas.
- The topics of study should allow for a time perspective (past, present and future).
(Kaplan, 1986, p. 186)

Process

Processes should include the types of skills the students will acquire through the learning experiences, such as:
- basic skills,
- research skills, and
- productive thinking skills.

The selection of the type of skill will depend upon the developmental level of the student and the specific learning needs to be addressed.

Product

The culmination of the learning experience is the product, although this may also be part of the learning experience, and it may exist in many forms across the disciplines from written to oral, to visual, to artistic, and so on.

LEARNING ENVIRONMENT

The lesson plans that are designed following the selection of the content, process and product, together with the organisation in the classroom, will influence the learning environment that develops. Kaplan (1986) described several factors inherent to the design of activities in order to promote the learning environment:
- students' developmental readiness;
- interest of students;
- characteristics of giftedness;
- availability of resources and time;
- type of gifted education program.

The following procedures developed by Dr Karen Rogers (1996–97), provide a useful structure for the development of a theme-based activity or unit of work using the Kaplan model.

Choose one key word, one concept and one or more disciplines within which you want to develop the unit.

Key words

There are twelve key words — and remember their related synonyms!

Kinds	Relationship	Types	Function
Conditions	Importance	Effects	Style
Changes	Characteristics	Purpose	Value

Concepts

There are an infinite number of these, including the following:

Power	Death	Leisure	Change
Ownership	Work	Courage	Life
Freedom	Commitment	Peace	Conflict
Family	Responsibility	Violence	Love
Invincibility	Sound	System	Religion
Hate	Creation	Silence	Wisdom
Morality	Evaluation	Energy	Friendship
Communication	Conservation	Pollution	Tradition
Emotion	Destruction	Law and order	Happiness
Understanding	Suffering	Truth	Knowledge
Supernatural issues	Beauty	Ignorance	Spirituality
Justice	Equality	Loyalty	Healing
Invention	Infinity	Evil	Immortality
Adaptation	Good	Tolerance	Exploration
Time	Fairness	Magic	Eternity
Education	Values	Survival	Growth

Disciplines

These could include domains such as economics, ecology, literature, law, history, as well as specific fields within a domain. Additionally, the development of a unit or an activity would include a list of basic skills, research skills and productive skills, along with the proposed conclusive product. The lists on the next pages outline some suggestions for each, but are by no means exhaustive.

Basic skills

Subject-based skills (outcomes) may also be included in this list:

Observing	Describing	Classifying
Following directions	Communicating	Designing investigations
Measuring	Sequencing	Generalising
Recognising relationships	Recording	Controlling variables
Inferring	Analysing	Making judgements
Organising graphs and charts	Using spatial relationships	Synthesising
Predicting	Hypothesising	

Research skills

Taking notes	Using a card catalogue
Using a classification key	Taking a survey
Interviewing	Observing detail through verbal or visual description
Using reference resources	Using journals, magazines, newspapers
Computerised bibliographic research	Writing abstracts
Reporting research	Analysing, interpreting data
Designing a research method	Outlining
Establishing criteria to judge	Substantiating with evidence
Using a retrieval system	Using fiction and nonfiction

Productive skills

1. Critical thinking skills

Evaluation/analysis

Verifiability	distinguish between verifiable facts or value claims.
Ambiguity	identify equivocal claims or ambiguity in argument.
Accuracy	determine the truthfulness of a statement.
Bias	determine the particular needs or stance of a source.
Induction	distinguish warranted or unwarranted conclusions.
Logic	recognise consistencies or inconsistencies in statements, conclusions or lines of reasoning.
Comprehensiveness	detect missing parts of argument; determine its strength.
Adequacy	judge whether a definition is adequate or appropriate.

Problem-solving

Definition	reduce problem to simple terms, workable elements; eliminate extraneous elements; identify central elements.
Information selection	distinguish between reliable and unreliable information sources; reject biased information; recognise relevant information.
Recognition of assumption	identify stated, unstated, relevant, irrelevant assumptions.
Hypothesising	discover clues to problem solution; select promising hypotheses; check hypotheses as opposed to information.
Concluding	draw valid conclusions; detect logical inconsistencies; recognise how to verify or judge adequacy of conclusions.

2. Creative thinking skills

Fluency	generate a large number of answers to an open question.
Flexibility	shift perspective or direction of thought easily.
Originality	generate a unique thought or product.
Elaboration	'improve' on simple ideas through detail.
Risk-taking	have courage to take a guess in ambiguous settings.
Curiosity	have willingness to toy with an idea of pure interest.
Divergent production	generate multiple original products, ideas, solutions.
Forecasting	predict plausible consequences based on given information.
Synectics	use metaphorical forms through personal, direct analogies.
Brainstorming	generate quantity of appropriate objects, ideas.
Forced relationships	find similarities between unlike objects, ideas.
Attribute listing	list inherent characteristics of idea or object.
Fantasy	generate non-real images for real or unreal ideas.
Imagery	generate visual images for real or unreal ideas.
Association	make connections; find relationships among objects or ideas.
Comparison	find similarities between objects or ideas.
Modification	change or reformulate ideas, problems or solutions.
Adaptation	use or apply object or idea in new context.
Magnification	go beyond what is usual to use objects in an exaggerated way.
Minification	focus on part of an object, idea or problem, and fully develop it.

CHAPTER 7

Substitution — generate alternative ideas or solutions to task, or problem.
Multiple uses — generate a number of uses for an object.
Rearrangement — shift, move around elements of an object, idea or problem.
Combination — add to idea or object by relating second idea or object.
Reversal — shift, transpose idea, object or problem to opposite.
Problem finding — find problem; detect gaps in information; ask good questions.
Fact finding — gather data in preparation for defining a problem.
Idea finding — generate, process, develop possible leads to a solution.
Solution finding — evaluate potential solutions against defined criteria.
Acceptance finding — develop a plan of action; implement chosen solution.

Products

Oral presentation	Value statement	Graphic representation
Self-evaluation	Editorial	Opinion
Debate	Story	Written report
Poem	Survey questionnaire	New game
Diagram	News article	Chart
News article	Advertisement	Cartoon
Model	Recipe	Illustration
Invention	Mobile	Television show
Map	Structure	Diorama
Puppet show	Sculpture	Pantomime
Set of photographs	Magazine	Puzzle
Simulation	Newspaper	Play
Book	Demonstration	Tape
Teaching lesson	Film strip	Computer program
Recommendation	Scrapbook	Letter
Research report	Journal	Exhibit
Panel discussion	Bulletin board	

The following matrices, known as Content–Process–Product (C–P–PR) Grids, are examples of the Kaplan model and a blank matrix is provided in the Appendix for you to use to design your own subject-specific unit.

65

■ CHAPTER 7

TABLE 11
KAPLAN C-P-PR GRID
HSIE/SOSE — EARLY STAGE 1 (KINDERGARTEN)
'ALL ABOUT ME'

THEME	BASIC SKILL	RESEARCH SKILL	PRODUCTIVE SKILL	PRODUCT
Families: Characteristics, similarities and differences.	Observing, following directions, measuring, recognising relationships, inferring, predicting.	Establishing criteria to judge, observing detail through verbal/visual description, analysing and interpreting data.	Recognition of assumptions, hypothesising, concluding, curiosity.	Photograph and picture display, oral presentation.

ARTICULATING ACTIVITY
Logical sequence of teaching this learning experience, incorporating all skills and product expectations to reflect on the 'theme'

Opening activity
- Whole-class discussion: important family occasions; celebrations in different cultures; family photographs.

Activities for identified gifted students:
- Sort and classify family photographs justifying the grouping strategies: How are they similar? How are they different?
- Create a display showing the customs of families in different cultures using photographs, illustrations and stories.

Activity
- Whole-class discussion: Who do I look like? How will I look when I am older?

Activities for identified gifted students:
- Survey the class and graph the height, hair and eye colours found.
- Predict and test whether other kindergarten classes have the same proportions of hair and eye colours in their students.
- Predict the height of the children in the class in five to ten years time if the children keep growing at the same rate. Do people continue to grow at the same rate throughout their lives? Why? Why not?
- Brainstorm how more could be found out about growth rates. What factors may influence a person's growth?
- Investigate family similarities and differences: Are thumbprints and fingerprints the same or different? Do people in the same family have the same fingerprints? What similarities can be found between the fingerprints on your hand? What about the hand of a family member? Do identical twins have the same fingerprints?
- Brainstorm how other body parts could be used to identify someone if they couldn't talk.
- Use high-powered magnifying glasses or a microscope to observe strands of hair and nail clippings. Discuss observations.
- Present all investigation predictions and findings to the class.

From Gross, MacLeod, Drummond and Merrick (2001) *Gifted Students in Primary Schools: Differentiating the Curriculum* Sydney: GERRIC.

**TABLE 12
KAPLAN C-P-PR GRID
HSIE/SOSE — STAGE 1 (YEARS 1 OR 2)
'PAST AND PRESENT'**

THEME	BASIC SKILL	RESEARCH SKILL	PRODUCTIVE SKILL	PRODUCT
Characteristics of family customs and traditions.	Recognising relationships, making judgements, recording, analysing.	Interviewing, analysing, interpreting data, establishing criteria to judge.	Draw valid conclusions.	Research: The past. Class museum. Birthday party. Report: What is history?

ARTICULATING ACTIVITY

Logical sequence of teaching this learning experience, incorporating all skills and product expectations to reflect on the 'theme'

Core learning experience
What is an oral history? Class investigations: how do we record history? Sharing of own past events, parent or grandparent stories of significant events in their lives, Aboriginal Dreamtime stories, traditional tales or stories from families or cultures.

Activities for identified gifted students:
- Explain oral history to a friend. Write a letter, tell a story or create a play.
- Record an oral history of your life. Include dates, chronological order, important milestones, humorous anecdotes.
- Develop a question about the past which interests you. Research the area of interest using books, CD-ROMs, the Internet, people and discussion with an 'expert' in this area. Present your research in a creative way.

Core learning experience
Class discussion: what relevant artefacts could be put in a time capsule which would represent today's schools and school children's lives?

Activities for identified gifted students:
- What artefact would you place in a time capsule which would best represent your family, its customs or traditions? In pairs, develop appropriate interview questions to discover information about this artefact. Interview a family member, recording the responses to the questions and report your findings to the class.
- Create a museum display of class artefacts. Use a grouping and classification system.

Core learning experience
Birthdays, past and present; family interviews about birthday celebrations. Interview a friend or parent to discover how they celebrate their birthday? How is this similar or different to the way you celebrate your birthday?

Activities for identified gifted students:
- Interview someone your own age, one of your parents or someone their age, and one of your grandparents or someone their age, to discover how they celebrate and celebrated birthdays as children. What was the same/different about the celebrations? How have birthday celebrations changed from past to present? Dramatise a birthday celebration from your parent's or grandparent's childhoods. Be careful to give an accurate representation of that era.
- Write an exposition: What is history?

From Gross, MacLeod, Drummond and Merrick (2001) *Gifted Students in Primary Schools: Differentiating the Curriculum* Sydney: GERRIC.

TABLE 13
KAPLAN C-P-PR GRID
HSIE/SOSE — STAGE 1 (YEARS 1 OR 2)
'ANCIENT CIVILISATIONS'

THEME	BASIC SKILL	RESEARCH SKILL	PRODUCTIVE SKILL	PRODUCT
Ancient civilisations: their importance to present day society.	Organising graphs and charts, recognising relationships, communicating.	Using reference sources, using a retrieval system, reporting research, using fiction and non-fiction.	Information selection, concluding.	Mind map of an ancient civilisation. Presentation of mind maps in order of existence of civilisations.

ARTICULATING ACTIVITY
Logical sequence of teaching this learning experience, incorporating all skills and product expectations to reflect on the 'theme'

Core activity
Pretest: short discussion about ancient civilisations centred on the story *Big Who. Little Stick* by Pamela Rogers. Students create a mind map to show knowledge of ancient civilisations. Students list what they would like to know on this topic.
In small groups, research information on a selected ancient civilisation, then create a mind map to show findings.

Activities for identified gifted students:
- In small groups, research a chosen ancient civilisation to discover customs, practices, symbols, languages and traditions along with social structure, dates and locations, beliefs, technology, clothing, food, arts, famous people, trade and reason for decline. Create a mind map to display findings.
- Compare the chosen ancient civilisation with its present-day counterpart or with our society. Discuss any similarities or differences between them. Devise a way to present the conclusions drawn.

Independent tasks for identified gifted students
Choose one of the following:
- What if the wheel had never been invented? Record your ideas in a creative way.
- How are ancient civilisations like our school?
- Pretend you are a child living in ancient Greece. Which of the Greek gods would you try to emulate and why? If you could interview this god, what would you ask him or her?
- After researching the topic of Roman architecture, write a lesson plan to teach your classmates about this.
- After reading different examples of guided imagery, develop a guided imagery text about a leaf floating in the breeze in ancient Pompeii.
- Write a children's book set in Inca times.

From Gross, MacLeod, Drummond and Merrick (2001) *Gifted Students in Primary Schools: Differentiating the Curriculum* Sydney: GERRIC.

CHAPTER 8
MODELS OF CURRICULUM DEVELOPMENT
WILLIAMS

WILLIAMS' COGNITIVE–AFFECTIVE INTERACTION MODEL

The Williams model is a design, rather than a theory, that assists teachers to offer a comprehensive learning experience in the classroom. The design is based on an acceptance that the school must address the needs of the 'whole child'. It also recognises that schools need to encourage higher-level thinking skills, including divergent and evaluative skills, in all students, but that encouraging these skills in gifted students is particularly crucial and that the products developed by gifted students should be of a qualitatively different level. The model is three-dimensional:

- **Dimension 1** is concerned with subject matter, where any subject matter normally found in the school curriculum can be included.
- **Dimension 2** is a list of eighteen teacher strategies that Williams believes stimulate positive learning behaviours. These strategies may be used with any content area, with the first eleven representing the strategies which are most ignored in schools yet which are the most appropriate for gifted students.
- **Dimension 3** involves eight creative processes which foster creative potential.

Many of Williams' teacher strategies may elicit a wide variety of student responses. For example, if a teacher presents an example of a paradox, the students who simply listen but do not engage with the idea may be operating on Bloom's knowledge level, but if they are truly processing and finding solutions for the contradictions involved, they may be exhibiting synthesis, flexibility, elaboration, complexity, originality and risk-taking (Rogers, 1997).

The Williams model may be implemented using a variety of methods to involve all three dimensions. These dimensions may be detailed as follows:

Cognitive — intellective behaviours

Fluency	generation of a quantity of relevant responses
Flexibility	variety of ideas or a shift in categories and directions of thought
Elaboration	embellishment or improvement of ideas; addition of details
Originality	unusual and/or unique ideas or responses; movement away from the obvious

Affective — temperament behaviours

Risk-taking	expose oneself to failure; take a guess; function in unstructured conditions
Curiosity	be inquisitive; toy with ideas; follow hunches; be open to puzzlement
Complexity	delve into intricate problems willingly; seek alternatives; see gaps
Imagination	visualise; build mental images; feel intuitively; reach beyond reality

Teaching strategies

Paradox
Statement or proposition which seems to be self-contradictory but may express a truth

Attribute listing
Inherent properties or identities that must be open-ended

Analogy
Finding similarities between things or situations which may in other ways be different

Discrepancy
Gaps or missing links in given knowledge

Provocative question
Inquiry to incite exploration and curiosity

Examples of change
Show the dynamics of things; make modifications, alterations or substitutions

Examples of habit
Build sensitivity to habit-bound thinking

Organised random search
Structured case study for new courses of action

Skills of search
Research on something done before; trial and error on new ways

Tolerance for ambiguity
Pose open-ended situations, e.g. 'What if ... ?'

Intuitive expression
Expressing emotion through the senses; guided imagery; role-playing

Adjustment to development
Examine or play back mistakes or failures

Study creative development
Analyse the traits of creative people; creative processes; or creative product

Evaluate situations
Extrapolate from ideas and actions; analyse implications or consequences

Creative reading skills
Generate novel ideas by reading

Creative listening skills
Generate novel ideas by listening

Creative writing skills
Generate novel ideas in writing

Visualisation
Express ideas in three-dimensional format or non-traditional formats

The following examples of activities based on the Williams models are subject specific and have been placed in a matrix format. A blank matrix is provided in the Appendix for you to use to design your own subject-specific unit.

CHAPTER 8

TABLE 14
WILLIAMS MODEL MATRIX
ENGLISH — STAGE 1 (YEARS 1 OR 2)
***WILFRED GORDON MCDONALD PARTRIDGE* BY MEM FOX**

PARADOX	What is unusual about the grandparents giving advice to a young boy?
ATTRIBUTE LISTING	List three of your earliest memories. What emotions do they bring with them?
ANALOGY	Why are memories as precious as gold? How is our memory like that of a computer?
DISCREPANCY	What would life be like if we had no memory? Explain at least five changes.
PROVOCATIVE QUESTION	It is sometimes thought that aged people lose their memories. Create a box full of items which would help you regain your memory when you are older.
EXAMPLES OF CHANGE	Choose one of the aged characters in the book. How does Wilfred's visit change that character?
EXAMPLES OF HABIT	What is a habit? Ask your grandparents or some older people you know if they have any habits, and how long they have had them. Predict any habits you may have when you are their age.
ORGANISED RANDOM SEARCH	Interview at least three different adults about their memories of childhood. Do these memories have any common elements? Group them under four different headings and present them in a creative way.
SKILLS OF SEARCH	How do we remember things? Design an experiment to test the memory of other students and trial it on a few of your classmates.
TOLERANCE FOR AMBIGUITY	What if your memory was wiped out after a sad event like the death of your favourite pet? What would be the consequence of that?
INTUITIVE EXPRESSION	What is your most treasured memory? Design and make, or collect, an item which defines that memory for you.
ADJUSTMENT TO DEVELOPMENT	Be a subject for another student's memory experiment. Did the experiment achieve its aim? Offer helpful suggestions on some ways the experiment might be improved.
STUDY CREATIVE PROCESS	Julie Vivas uses watercolour in this book. Create an artwork in watercolour titled 'Memory'.
EVALUATE SITUATIONS	What do you do when you can't remember where you have put something? Is there a better way to do this?
CREATIVE READING SKILLS	Read two other books by Mem Fox. How are these books similar and different?
CREATIVE LISTENING SKILLS	Invite an older person who attended your school as a child to talk to your class. What are his or her memories of your school? How have things changed and stayed the same?
CREATIVE WRITING SKILLS	Write a letter to an aged person you know. Include some news of your own and ask some questions about that person's memories.
VISUALISATION	Help to plan and create a mural for your class based on the book.

From Gross, MacLeod, Drummond and Merrick (2001) *Gifted Students in Primary Schools: Differentiating the Curriculum* Sydney: GERRIC.

**TABLE 15
WILLIAMS MODEL MATRIX
SCIENCE — STAGE 2 (YEARS 3 OR 4)
'SIMPLE MACHINES'**

PARADOX	Discuss the statement: 'Machines! Can't live with them, can't live without them!'
ATTRIBUTE LISTING	List the simple machines which are used on a building site.
ANALOGY	How is a lever like a friend?
DISCREPANCY	Were simple machines found in all of the ancient cultures? Why? Why not?
PROVOCATIVE QUESTION	Would we have been better off without 'Game Boys'? Why?
EXAMPLES OF CHANGE	How did the invention of scissors change our lives?
EXAMPLES OF HABIT	The electricity goes off in your house for a week. How does this affect your household and what do you do to cope?
ORGANISED RANDOM SEARCH	Study and explain alternative sources of energy used to drive machinery.
SKILLS OF SEARCH	Choose an inventor who has 'changed the world'. What motivated him or her and what were the ideas?
TOLERANCE FOR AMBIGUITY	What would the world be like if one of the simple machines had not been invented? Choose one and explain your ideas.
INTUITIVE EXPRESSION	Which simple machine are you most like and why?
ADJUSTMENT TO DEVELOPMENT	Design a toy for a young child using only simple machines. Make the toy and trial it with students in Year 1. Redesign, if necessary.
STUDY CREATIVE PROCESS	Investigate competitions and awards for inventors. What sorts of inventions win these events?
EVALUATE SITUATIONS	How important is computer technology to the development and use of machines? Explain using one machine as an example.
CREATIVE READING SKILLS	Choose two different information books about simple machines. Decide which one is more effective in its explanations and presentation. Explain your choice.
CREATIVE LISTENING SKILLS	Interview an inventor to discover when and why he or she became interested in inventing new things or ideas, and what he or she is working on currently.
CREATIVE WRITING SKILLS	Write a humorous story for younger readers about an inventor whose new invention did not turn out the way he or she expected.
VISUALISATION	Design a machine for the year 2100 which will improve communication.

From Gross, MacLeod, Drummond and Merrick (2001) *Gifted Students in Primary Schools: Differentiating the Curriculum* Sydney: GERRIC.

TABLE 16
WILLIAMS MODEL MATRIX
MATHEMATICS — STAGE 3 (YEARS 5 OR 6)
'WHY WAS PYTHAGORAS IMPORTANT?'

PARADOX	It is said that mathematics and music are interrelated. How is this so?
ATTRIBUTE LISTING	Pythagoras and the 'Brotherhood' developed the theory of number. What main theories did they devise?
ANALOGY	How is a world without number like a world without colour?
DISCREPANCY	Why did the 'Brotherhood' use the five-pointed star as their symbol of recognition?
PROVOCATIVE QUESTION	The motto of the Pythagoreans was: 'All is number'. What did they mean?
EXAMPLES OF CHANGE	The 'Brotherhood' discovered irrational numbers which led to the realisation that 'all is not number'. How did the Pythagoreans explain this?
EXAMPLES OF HABIT	Pythagoras tried in vain to discover a way to 'square a circle'. Has a solution to 'squaring the circle' been discovered?
ORGANISED RANDOM SEARCH	Who were the members of the Pythagorean 'Brotherhood'?
SKILLS OF SEARCH	There are several ways of generating numbers known as 'Pythagorean Triples'. Discover some of these.
TOLERANCE FOR AMBIGUITY	What would happen to our number system if there were no zero?
INTUITIVE EXPRESSION	Pretend you are Pythagoras and you have discovered prime numbers. Describe how you would explain this to the 'Brotherhood'.
ADJUSTMENT TO DEVELOPMENT	The 'Brotherhood' could not solve the problem of 'squaring the circle'. How did Hippocrates attempt to solve this problem?
STUDY CREATIVE PROCESS	What is the work of a mathematician in current times?
EVALUATE SITUATIONS	Do you consider the work of the 'Brotherhood' in mathematics significant? Explain your opinion.
CREATIVE READING SKILLS	Read the information book: *Pythagoras & His Theorem* by Paul Strathern. After reading the book, develop ten questions you would like to ask Pythagoras if you were able to interview him.
CREATIVE LISTENING SKILLS	Invite a mathematician to talk to your class about his or her work. Discover what he or she believes is important about mathematics.
CREATIVE WRITING SKILLS	Rewrite a fairytale so that there is no reference to numbers.
VISUALISATION	A pentagram can be traced by drawing over the lines with a pencil without lifting the pencil off the paper and without tracing any line more than once. Investigate any other designs, patterns or shapes for which this is possible.

From Gross, MacLeod, Drummond and Merrick (2001) *Gifted Students in Primary Schools: Differentiating the Curriculum* Sydney: GERRIC.

CHAPTER 9
INDEPENDENT RESEARCH PROJECTS

Independent research projects are, exactly as the name implies, research projects which are independent and student-centred. Treffinger (1986) defines independent learning as self-directed work on problems for which the individual has ownership. 'Ownership entails *influence* (being capable of and responsible for action on a problem), *interest* (personal involvement in the task and concern for action about the problem) and *imagination* (opportunity for and acceptance of new ideas)' (Treffinger, 1986, p. 431). It is important to bear in mind that independent research projects are not specifically the domain of gifted education and that the concept of independent research is certainly beneficial for all students. However, the opportunity for gifted students to investigate in depth over an extended period of time a topic or a question in an area of passion responds to many of the characteristics and needs of gifted students such as those described in Chapter 2.

Specifically, independent research projects address the gifted students' needs for:
- opportunities to pursue individual interests;
- contact with experts;
- long-term projects;
- theme-based work;
- individualised and advanced reading;
- moving beyond the core curriculum;
- developing organisational strategies;
- developing goal-setting abilities;
- encouraging intellectual risk-taking;
- exposure to other viewpoints;
- problem solving in the affective domain;
- discussion of values and morals;
- philosophy;
- mentoring.

Who should engage in an independent research project?

Children of all ages and all abilities benefit from engaging in research projects. Betts (1986) states that the primary goal for each learner who participates in this type of project is the attainment of autonomous learning skills. These learning skills are based on the learner's ability to develop new ideas and projects with minimal guidance and, as such, relate to the student's developmental level rather than his or her chronological age. These projects allow for the establishment of goals which are specific to the needs of gifted students, and include:
- developing more positive concepts of self;
- comprehending their own giftedness in relation to self and society;
- developing the skills necessary to interact with peers, parents and other adults;
- increasing their knowledge in a variety of subject areas;
- developing their thinking, decision-making and problem-solving skills;
- participating in activities designed to facilitate and integrate the individual's cognitive, emotional and social development;
- demonstrating responsibility for their own learning in and out of the school setting;
- becoming responsible, creative, independent learners.

(Betts, 1986, p. 32)

What are the logistics of independent research?

Independent research projects can be organised in a wide variety of ways. However, as the main purpose is to provide an opportunity for in-depth and long-term study, it is important that the time span of the project responds to this need. Generally, the majority of research projects will extend over at least one term and in the later stages of primary school over two terms. Students will need to be allocated a block of time each week to work on their projects, preferably no less than 90 minutes (usually an afternoon block from lunch onwards is the most workable option). As discussed in Chapter 2, academically gifted students usually have a long attention span and value the opportunity for sustained, long-term engagement.

Students working on independent research will also need the opportunity to utilise resources which may not be found in the regular classroom. Regular and ongoing access to the library is essential. Flexible timetabling and consultation with the teacher librarian should allow this to function successfully and with minimal disruption to the rest of the school community.

Who decides the topics or questions for research?

The decision as to the topic or theme to be studied should arise from a negotiation process between the student, the teacher or facilitator and the parent or parents (or caregivers). Students may initially identify several themes or topics of interest to them and brainstorm possible research areas for each. It is at this stage that the teacher or facilitator may meet with the student to discuss his or her ideas and guide the process of narrowing down and refining the choices. It is extremely important that the concept or topic be an area of passion for the student as it will become difficult to maintain interest and enthusiasm over an extended period if this is not the case.

Once the choice of a concept or topic has been finalised, the next stage involves the formulation of a research question. The following are examples of concepts, topics and focus questions chosen by students in Year 6 at MLC School, Burwood, NSW:

Theme:	Topic:	Focus question:
Change	Animals	Is horse racing ethically, morally and financially acceptable in Australia?
	Genetics	How and why is food genetically modified?
	Medicine	Can beauty be achieved through a surgeon's knife?
	Revolution	Who won the French Revolution?
	Astronomy	How has technology changed our view of the universe in the 20th century?
	Technology	How has technology changed photography?
Mind	Psychology	How do we sleep? What happens if we don't sleep? What are dreams? How do we remember? Do we all have psychic powers?
Beliefs	Astronomy	Why was astronomy important to the ancient Egyptians?
	Myths and legends	How do Aboriginal creation myths differ from those of the Aztecs?
	Art and religion	How did Chinese artists of the Ming Dynasty portray their religion?
	Truth and illusion	Are there such creatures as fairies?
Freedom	Democracy	Does democracy ensure freedom?
	Heroes	What is a hero?
Nature	Photography	How does photography impact on the preservation of our environment in Australia?
Models	Architecture	How might future housing in Australia benefit the environment?
Tyranny	Music	Why did Hitler ban some composers and their music during the Third Reich?
Infinity	Astronomy	Is there an end to space?
Humanity	Technology	Is 'Number 5' alive?
	Politics	Should Australia have the death penalty?

What types of research can be conducted?

Starko and Schack (1994) describe five different types of research particularly appropriate to primary school students:
- descriptive, e.g. public opinion surveys, census studies, descriptive observations, consumer research and analysis of test data;
- historical, e.g. newspaper interviews with famous people about their work, diaries, magazine articles about past events, interviews with parents or grandparents, investigation of music lyrics from the past;

- experimental, e.g. scientific or medical studies which involve the manipulation of variables and the investigation of cause and effect relationships;
- correlational, e.g. the investigation of the relationships among variables and the magnitude of the positive or negative relationship; and
- developmental, e.g. the investigation of the changes and patterns of growth over time in longitudinal and cross-sectional studies.

Who is the audience? What assessment tools are appropriate?

It is important that gifted students are given the opportunity to present their research projects to an audience who are not only able to understand the content of the project but who are also experts in the fields of research. Presentations to peers should be to intellectual rather than chronological peers. Adults who have been invited to be members of a panel should be informed as to the nature of the project the students have undertaken, the criteria set for evaluation and the outcomes expected. If possible, an evaluation outline should be given to them as a model for responding to the presentation. Additionally, it is useful for a question and answer time to be appended to each presentation to allow for the panel to gain further insight into the depth of understanding of the topic. This session should not be lengthy but should allow each student to respond to questions and to explain, in a less formal manner, anything not covered in the formal presentation. The following is a suggested evaluation guide for panel members:

EVALUATION GUIDE FOR INDEPENDENT RESEARCH PROJECT PANEL PRESENTATION

The student should:
- clearly link the theme, concept and focus question in each component;
- show clear evidence of organisation and focus;
- show clear understanding of the focus question chosen;
- use proper enunciation, volume, inflection and tone;
- utilise eye contact and body language;
- use vocabulary appropriate to the area of research;
- use visual aids and technology to enhance the presentation;
- communicate ideas clearly and creatively;
- show effort, thought and scholarship in each component;
- display original thought and expression;
- respond confidently to questions posed by the panel;
- demonstrate higher-level thinking skills, e.g. analysis, synthesis and evaluation of information presented;
- demonstrate the use of multiple sources in the research project;
- validate information based on credibility, accuracy and logic;
- draw conclusions and/or make predictions about cause and effect relationships.

Starko and Schack (1994) suggest that the provision of the real audience may require the invitation of adults outside the school community and that if the number of student researchers presenting allows it, a student research conference may be more appropriate. As with professional conferences, 'student researchers submit proposals for research presentations which are then timetabled for specific times and locations, with several presentations occurring simultaneously. Those attending the research conference receive a program and select from the presentations available at a given time slot' (Starko and Schack, 1994, p. 115).

What are the stages of the project?

- Selection of students to participate
- Meeting with students, teachers or facilitators and parents or caregivers
- Brainstorming possible topics, questions or problems
- Negotiation of focus question relating to chosen theme or topic
- Outlining the guidelines for the required components for research and presentation
- Negotiation of learning outcomes
- Designing format of research portfolio, e.g. those materials which are collected and collated throughout the research process which are in hard-copy format, such as written documents and photographs
- Designing format of research presentation
- Setting timeline for completion of components, including assigned meeting times with teacher or facilitator
- Conducting research; develop set components of project
- Submission of components by negotiated set dates
- Presentation to panel of experts and/or research conference
- Evaluation by all participants

AN EXAMPLE OF AN INDEPENDENT STUDY PROJECT

Special note. This unit is based on an Advanced Placement (AP) English unit developed for senior students by Lori Koplik and Cheryl Gherardini from Rhode Island, United States of America. This may be located at http://www.cogeco.ca/~rayser/indstdy.txt. Lori Koplik and Cheryl Gherardini have kindly given permission for their work to be modified for the purpose of this book.

Introduction

During this term/semester, you will have the opportunity to create an independent multimedia project which is research based, and which answers a focus question you have chosen or designed.

The first stage of your research should involve your proposal, outlining your theme, focus question and how you intend to present your research. During the term/semester, you will meet with your teacher or facilitator on several predetermined occasions to ensure you are meeting your goals and the project outcomes. The final stage of your research will be a presentation of your work to a panel of experts and your peers. The panel will consist of adults who are expert in the field of study you have chosen, or who have a passionate interest in this field.

Presentations

What is a presentation? A presentation may be viewed, in its simplest terms, as an advanced show-and-tell in which you demonstrate:
- your complete immersion in your chosen area of focus, and
- that you have learned something worthwhile. Since one student's focus may be vastly different from that of others, the presentations may vary somewhat in form or emphasis.

However, all presentations should:
- contain the *five* required components;
- *tie components together thematically*. Remember to make clear how each component relates to your theme;
- utilise some *physical format for display*, such as a poster, a bulletin board, an album or a portfolio; this should display some or all of the required components and should be worked into the presentation;
- *demonstrate* diligence, creativity and scholarship;
- last about *fifteen minutes.*

CHAPTER 9

Core requirements

Each of you will complete the following core requirements. It is up to you to determine how each of these components can be best shaped to develop, define and illustrate your subject. Some suggestions are listed below each component; there are other possibilities which may better suit specific cases.

Presentation components

1. **Research component** (several sources cited):
    - history, origin, causes of ...
    - criticism, essays written about ...
    - recent developments, events in ...
    - statistics, studies about ...
    - social, political, economic problems which illustrate...
    - your own original research to support or negate other research (this *must* be negotiated with your teacher or facilitator prior to commencement!)

2. **Writing component** (choose two from different genres):
    - Creative writing: parody, newspaper, 'how-to' booklet, short story, poem, monologue
    - Exposition: define, analyse, argue, persuade
    - Journal: keep an ongoing reaction and progress journal during the independent study; record your feelings about the subject, or document your progress as you work
    - Letter: write a letter to someone you love (or like) telling about your experience in detail — and send it

3. **Fine arts component:**
Find or create and perform or share with the class:
    - music
    - art
    - video
    - theatre
    - photography
    - dance ... or other alternative means of expression

    Please provide some *explanation* for your choice and its relevance to your focus.

4. Literary component:

Read some fiction on the subject. Find a book, a short story or a play which deals directly or indirectly with your subject. Take *informal notes* or keep a *reaction journal*. Your notes will be submitted with any other 'hard copy' on the day of your presentation.

5. Multimedia component:

Design a multimedia presentation to utilise whilst presenting to the panel of experts. This may involve a slide show, a Web-page design or any other negotiated software. It should include the following:
- graphics (clip art, digitised images, personally created graphics, scanned images)
- sound (imported sounds, digitised sounds)
- video clips (if available or possible)
- transitions
- buttons (for self-guided tours!!!)
- clear text (informative, but preferably in point form)
- thoughtful and creative design

Note. Please remember to acknowledge your sources and to use only clip art, sound clips or video clips which are free to use.

Criteria for self-evaluation

It is important that as you work, you constantly refer to the following criteria to guide your efforts:
- **Coherence.** Is theme clearly stated? Are components thematically connected? Does narration continually reinforce theme?
- **Depth.** Does each component reflect effort, thought and scholarship?
- **Diligence.** Did you work hard all throughout the process?
- **Creativity.** Does your presentation reflect original thought and expression? Did your research propel you into new territory?

You will be given an opportunity to submit your self-evaluation at the conclusion of your panel presentation. Additionally, you should negotiate with your teacher or facilitator which learning outcomes you will be meeting throughout your work. These may vary from student to student but should be submitted to the panel prior to your presentation.

Themes

The following list of themes or concepts may help you decide the focus of your research project. For example, you may be interested in the topic 'Infinity' and want to research the question: 'Do all languages have the term "infinity" and does it always mean the same thing?' or alternatively, you may choose 'Heroism' and ask the question 'What is a hero?'. Regardless of what theme or concept you choose, a focus question must be designed to guide your research, to prevent the topic becoming too vast to complete in the allocated time.

Power	Death	Leisure	Change
Ownership	Work	Courage	Life
Freedom	Commitment	Peace	Conflict
Family	Responsibility	Violence	Love
Invincibility	Sound	System	Religion
Hate	Creation	Silence	Wisdom
Morality	Evaluation	Energy	Friendship
Communication	Conservation	Pollution	Tradition

CHAPTER 9

Emotion	Destruction	Law and order	Happiness
Understanding	Suffering	Truth	Knowledge
Supernatural issues	Beauty	Ignorance	Spirituality
Justice	Equality	Loyalty	Healing
Invention	Infinity	Evil	Immortality
Adaptation	Good	Tolerance	Exploration
Time	Fairness	Magic	Eternity
Education	Values	Survival	Growth

Alternatively, you may prefer to choose a topic from the following list:

Advertising	Animals	Archeology	Architecture
Art and artists	Astronomy	Authors	Biology
Careers	Chemistry	Communication	Computers
Conservation	Ecology	Economics	Energy
Etymology	Legends and myths	Future	Genealogy
Genetics	Geology	Geography	Medicine
Music	Nutrition	Oceanography	Phobias
Photography	Pollution	Senior citizens	Sign language

EXAMPLE: INDEPENDENT RESEARCH STUDY PROPOSAL SHEET
PAGE 1

Name:_____

Note. This is an initial proposal. Actual components may change course as you dig deeper into the topic. The proposal is just to get you focused.

1. Idea of focus:

   a. Theme or concept:

   b. Focus question:

2. Research component (explain specifically what you intend to research, including any original research you intend to conduct):

3. Writing components (explain specific form and focus of two):

   1.

   2.

4. Fine arts component (explain specific form and focus):

5. Literary component (if you have a title at present, please provide it; if not, describe the type of reading you would like to do):

■ CHAPTER 9

**EXAMPLE: INDEPENDENT RESEARCH STUDY
PROPOSAL SHEET
PAGE 2**

Name:_____

6. Multimedia component (explain software to be used and ideas to be presented):

7. Please list any unusual resources or logistics which your project may entail. For example, will your work take you outside of the classroom? Why? For how long? Will you need supplies of any kind? How do you plan to get them?

8. What display format do you intend to use?

9. When will you meet with your teacher or facilitator to discuss your progress?

   Meeting 1 date:

   Meeting 2 date:

   Meeting 3 date:

_____   _____   _____
Your signature   Parent's or   Teacher's or
                                caregiver's signature   facilitator's signature

Date: _____

CHAPTER 10
DEVELOPING UNITS OF WORK

Following identification, off-level testing and pretesting, it is important to design appropriate units of work to meet the required objectives for the topic, or to extend the student's skills and understanding beyond the core curriculum. A teacher may decide to use one specific curriculum model or a combination of several models, depending on the objectives needed to be achieved. Regardless of the model chosen or the subject area involved, the following steps are helpful when designing a unit of work.

Note. All examples given in this chapter are designed for Stage 3 (Years 5 or 6).

CHAPTER 10

RATIONALE

The rationale for a unit of work places the unit and its activities into the specific context of the students and class involved. It provides a brief overview of the teacher's aims throughout the unit and is primarily a statement of purpose.

EXAMPLE: RATIONALE FROM INTERDISCIPLINARY UNIT 'OUR CHANGING PLANET' (SEE CHAPTER 12)

Since its beginning, the world has been constantly changing. Humankind's presence on the timeline of this change has been both comparatively recent and short in duration. However, the effect of this presence has dramatically altered the previously natural progression of this planet.

The primary purpose of this unit is to study the changes that have occurred and are still occurring to our planet, both physically and environmentally. By investigating humankind's effects on these elements, students can evaluate human intervention and predict future possibilities.

This is a multidisciplinary unit that is underpinned by the development of critical and creative thinking skills. Students are encouraged to become active learners by completing a wide range of activities both in class, group and individual structures.

Through the provision of opportunities to interact with their intellectual peers, gifted students will be encouraged to demonstrate the development of their abilities in the higher-order thinking skills of analysis, synthesis and evaluation by working at a faster pace and higher level of cognitive reasoning.

EXAMPLE: RATIONALE FROM ENGLISH UNIT 'THROUGH THE WARDROBE DOOR'

> High fantasy is characterised by a secondary world setting, an 'Everyman' protagonist, strong characterisation, a quest, the struggle between good and evil, value laden events and ideas, and an overriding theme concerned with supernatural elements or nonrational phenomena. Paradoxically, good fantasy uses these elements to put readers more closely in touch with reality. Fantasy expresses reality in a way that realistic fiction cannot, through the language of the inner self. Because high fantasy appeals to the inner self, it is an ideal genre to stimulate creative responses from students. (Cullinan, 1987)

In early childhood, most children read or are told fairytales that possess, at a basic level, many elements which exist in fantasy literature. In fairytales, fantastic settings and strange creatures are commonplace and a variety of moral issues are usually portrayed. Children learn to transfer such values as the measures of honesty, courage, fairness, inventiveness and acceptance from these tales to their everyday lives.

The study of the elements of fantasy literature builds on the assumed experiences of gifted students during their earlier encounters with fairytales. The primary purpose of this unit is to study and evaluate the elements that define particular novels as pertaining to the fantasy style. This unit not only looks at setting, characterisation and theme, but delves further to examine the plot, style and background of novels written in this genre. Students will be encouraged to relate the themes and values found in these narratives to their own personal experiences, and to become active participants on discussions and group activities.

The activities in this unit will foster independent learning experiences and students will be encouraged to demonstrate cooperation and collaborative interaction with their academic peers.

OUTCOMES

The outcomes of a unit of work should be linked to the outcomes prescribed in the appropriate syllabus for that subject. Treffinger, Hohn and Feldhusen (1989) summarised the characteristics of useful outcomes, also described as objectives, as follows:
- A useful outcome gives a clear statement of the important learning that should occur as a result of instruction.
- The learning outcome is described using words that describe student behaviour as explicitly as possible.
- A useful outcome is clear and unambiguous, and avoids, as much as possible, language that is open to many interpretations, such as 'to know', 'to understand' or 'to appreciate'.
- A useful outcome states the kinds of observable performance that will show that the student has mastered the outcome.

EXAMPLE: OUTCOMES FROM ENGLISH UNIT 'SCIENCE FICTION, FUTURE REALITY?'

During this unit, students will:
- compare and contrast two novels by the same author;
- complete a biographical sketch or 'bio-board' of that author;
- respond to literature using interpretative, critical and evaluative processes;
- create a Web site to share: the 'compare and contrast' essays about the novels written by students in the class, their biographical sketches of their chosen author, and databases of their chosen author's works;
- compare the authenticity of the science fiction issues found in fictional texts with those found in print and visual media.

EXAMPLE: OUTCOMES FROM ENGLISH/HSIE INTERDISCIPLINARY UNIT 'TO BE OR NOT TO BE: A STUDY OF EMINENCE'

As a result of this unit, students will be able to:

Content:
- recognise the themes, character development, symbolism and settings in the examples of classic literature they read;
- identify an eminent author's purpose and audience;
- identify the devices of emotion, intuition and aesthetics;
- use historical background and author biographies to explain the general structures of classic literature;
- develop a definition of 'giftedness' through the research and portrayal of an eminent person;
- compare the life of an eminent person to their own life.

Process:
- make inferences based on information from novels;
- evaluate their feelings and reactions to the novels they have read whilst comparing different works;
- identify the universality of themes in this genre;
- use the skills of analysis, synthesis and evaluation to respond to set and free-choice tasks;
- develop research skills by utilising both primary and secondary resources in writing biographies, autobiographies and 'bio-riddles';
- work independently.

Product:
- demonstrate competency in the writing process;
- use multiple sources in preparing research reports;
- organise an effective presentation;
- demonstrate knowledge of an eminent person during the presentation.

Learning environment:
- work cooperatively in group and whole-class situations;
- evaluate group and peer performance based on a set of predetermined criteria;
- understand, practise and demonstrate skills, concepts, and attitudes for lifelong learning.

CONTENT OUTLINE

Developing a written content outline for a unit of work highlights several valuable factors:
- It allows the teacher to ensure that core content is covered.
- It allows the design of extension beyond the core for the gifted students within a particular class.
- It provides an opportunity to observe any areas in the unit design which may be under- or over-represented.

The content outline may be written in point form or as a concept web or map, as seen in the following examples:

EXAMPLE: CONTENT OUTLINE FROM INTERDISCIPLINARY UNIT 'OUR CHANGING PLANET' (SEE CHAPTER 12)

A. English:
1. Accessing text: fiction and nonfiction
2. Response to literature
3. Creative writing: poetry and narrative; drama script
4. Talking and listening: debate and prepared speech
5. Exposition: letter writing; essays

B. Science and technology:
1. Geological timeline
2. Basics of palaeontology
3. Experiments in plate tectonics
4. Aquatic field study
5. Current health issues linked to global warming (links to PD, Health, & PE)

C. HSIE:
1. Patterns of human involvement
2. Environment: natural patterns of change — affects and response
3. Case study

D. Creative and practical arts:
1. Drama: utilisation of dramatic element in group presentation
2. Music: use of music to portray environmental themes
3. Dance: utilise dance element in group presentation; use of dance to portray environmental themes
4. Visual Arts: painting; sketching; sculpture; mural; models; printing

CHAPTER 10

**EXAMPLE: CONCEPT WEB
INTERDISCIPLINARY UNIT
'OUR CHANGING PLANET'**

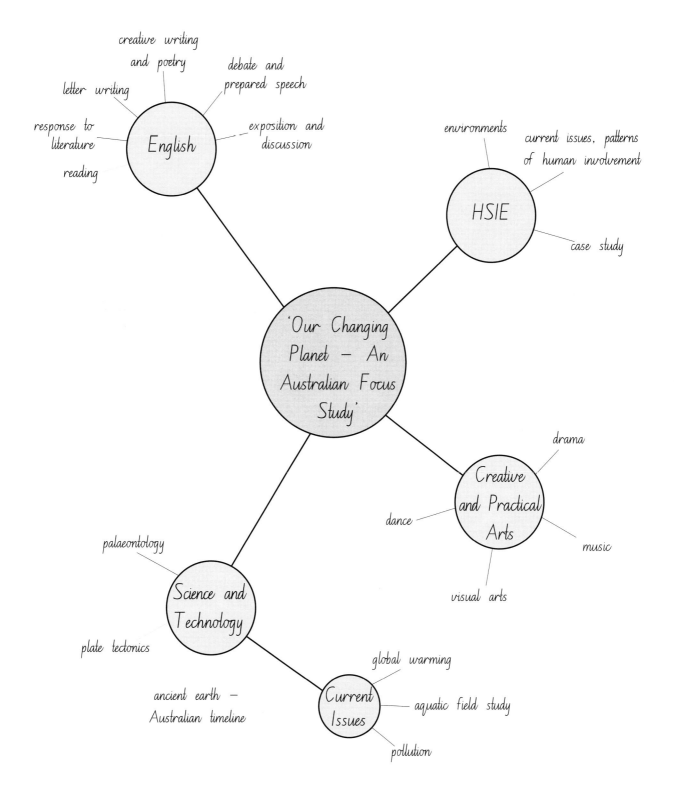

89

CHAPTER 10

**EXAMPLE: CONCEPT WEB
ENGLISH UNIT
'THROUGH THE WARDROBE DOOR'**

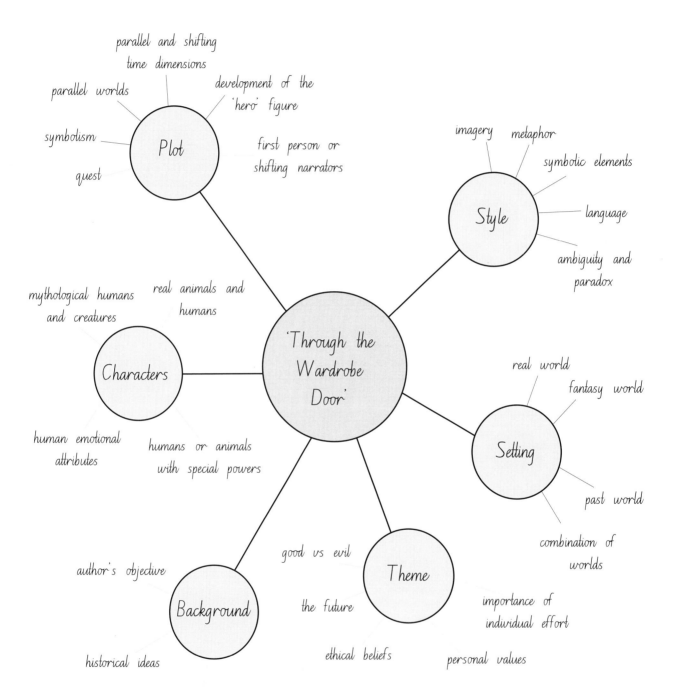

CHAPTER 10

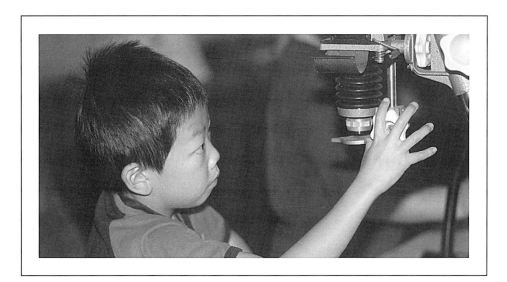

USING A MATRIX

An alternative way of outlining the content and focus questions of a unit is to create a matrix. A matrix is usually based on content and process modifications, with product modifications being included in the actual presentation of each activity (see Chapter 5). The headings in the content row and process column should relate to the specific outcomes desired for each unit in respect to the gifted students in the class.

Once the matrix is completed, the activities designed may be incorporated within the framework of the entire unit, being used as individual and/or group tasks as appropriate. The table on the next page demonstrates an example of a matrix in the key learning area of English.

TABLE 17
UNIT MATRIX
ENGLISH – STAGE 3 (YEARS 5 OR 6)
NOVEL STUDY

INDIVIDUAL SET TASKS	PLOT	CHARACTERS	THEMES
APPLICATION	Do problems in the story resemble problems in your life?	Do the characters in the story learn things about life which are true and important?	Did anything in this story really make you think? Why?
ANALYSIS	What stages of development does the protagonist go through? Explain with examples.	Are there different types of characters? Describe what makes them different.	Are there several points of view in the story?
SYNTHESIS	Does the story remind you of other stories you have read? How and why?	Is there a character in the story who could be removed without affecting the plot? Why? Why not?	Does the title of the story help to tie the story together? How?
EVALUATION	Is the plot believable? Should it be?	Who was your favourite character? Why?	Is the story well written? Explain.
DIVERGENCE	If you were the author, what changes would you make to the story?	Is there anything about any of the characters in the story you would change? Why?	How else could the book have ended?
INTUITION	What images are strongest in your mind when you remember the story?	Was your first impression about the personality of the protagonist correct? Explain.	What events in the story remind you of your own life?
EMOTION	What was the strongest emotion you felt when you read the story? Why?	Which character are you most similar to emotionally?	Did you laugh or cry? Why? At what places or events in the story?
ETHICS	Are any of the characters placed in situations which make it difficult to know what is right?	Have any of the characters shown moral courage?	How do the characters in the story decide what is right?
AESTHETICS	How do colours, sounds and other sensations contribute to the power of certain scenes in the story?	Who was the most 'colourful' character in the story?	Would you describe any of the scenes as particularly beautiful or ugly? Why?

From Gross, MacLeod, Drummond and Merrick (2001) *Gifted Students in Primary Schools: Differentiating the Curriculum* Sydney: GERRIC.

CHAPTER 11
EVALUATING UNITS OF WORK

n essential step in the process of curriculum development is a well-planned and effective process of evaluation. We need to check that both the content of a curriculum unit and the teaching and learning strategies we are employing are working effectively. The procedures for evaluating any particular unit of work should be devised at the same time that the unit objectives, outcomes and activities are being designed, and not left as an ad hoc process or afterthought. Two types of evaluation are involved: assessment of student progress; and assessment of curriculum effectiveness (Maker, 1982):

- **Student progress.** This type of evaluation may occur both in informal contexts such as peer appraisal and self-evaluation and in formal contexts such as pre- and post-tests, or standardised tests.
- **Curriculum effectiveness.** This should ideally be an ongoing form of assessment and involve teacher lesson logs and anecdotal records, student post-unit questionnaires, and outside perceptions of the curriculum, such as parent responses.

The following examples of unit evaluation demonstrate teacher and parent responses to the implementation of particular units of work.

EXAMPLE: TEACHER EVALUATION
ENGLISH UNIT — STAGE 3 (YEARS 5 OR 6)
'THROUGH THE WARDROBE DOOR'

'This unit was far more rigorous in content than any I have planned for in past mixed ability classes I have taught. As this was a self-contained gifted class, my aim was to include more opportunities for synthesis and evaluation activities, whilst also allowing the students the opportunity for choice. The lessons took longer than I first planned, and the students seem to also take longer to complete individual tasks than I had envisaged they would. However, the depth to which they took each task was also far beyond my original expectations. It was interesting to observe the group tasks and note the ability of different members of the group to cooperate, negotiate and lead.

'All of the lessons and activities planned for this unit were product orientated, although the products were rarely specified in any detail. In most cases the students were given suggestions for products but they generally created their own ideas. The students were given the opportunity to present their work, individually and in groups, to their peers and to an invited audience of parents and other students on a presentation day.

'This unit had very little teacher talk emphasis and student discussions rarely had me as the central focus. I enjoyed this aspect of the unit and I found myself learning along with the students. Some of the students struggled to work independently at the start of the unit but as the unit progressed and these particular students observed their peers working independently, this seemed to lessen as a problem.

'Providing flexibility of schedule was very difficult in my particular school situation and both the students and I experienced frustrations in this area. We began the beginning of the term by deciding as a team how we would timetable lessons during the week to allow more "unit" time. The students set aside "group times", "research times", "access to the Internet" times, and so on. However, this did not always work as planned, as interruptions occurred.

'Planning this unit of work has led me to do the same for a unit in HSIE (Human Society and Its Environment) and in Science and Technology. I would like to now work on units that are more interdisciplinary in structure than intradisciplinary, in an attempt to alleviate some of the frustrations of timetabling that occur.'

EXAMPLE: TEACHER EVALUATION
LITERATURE UNIT — STAGE 3 (YEARS 5 OR 6)
'PERSONAL CHANGE'

'This unit worked well despite the substantial rise in the students' standards of reading required by the complex novels in the unit. The identified gifted students who participated enjoyed the personal research task's demand on their reading ability, which culminated in some excellent presentations to the class. The individualisation of many of the tasks was very important as the students were at such different levels of ability. Many of the tasks required far more time than was available as the students became so involved and focused in specific areas, especially the topic of "persecution". The group tasks were effective, allowing even those students who usually avoid group activities, a chance to participate successfully.'

EXAMPLE: PARENT EVALUATIONS
ENGLISH/HSIE INTERDISCIPLINARY UNIT — STAGE 3 (YEARS 5 OR 6)
'TO BE OR NOT TO BE: A STUDY OF EMINENCE'

These were collected after student presentations to an adult audience.

'A message from an adult procrastinator — congratulations on getting your ISPs (Independent Study Project) together so successfully, whether at the last minute or not. Future research tasks and projects will come all the more easily and enjoyably. A really interesting evening!'

'This was a wonderful presentation. The talent and dedication of this group to their projects is highly commended. Well done! This was a good learning experience for the students as well as the parents.'

'We were surprised and enchanted by the breadth and depth of the different presentations. The styles were stimulating and of course, the multimedia presentations were stunning. We encourage you all to continue with such high standards of work. Well done!'

The following forms provide a variety of evaluation tools which may be used during and at the conclusion of a unit of work in most subject areas.

EXAMPLE: INDIVIDUAL RESEARCH TASK TEACHER EVALUATION FORM

Name: _____

Task: _____

1 Experiencing difficulty
2 Developing
3 Competent
4 Highly developed

Content:

1. The research task addresses the main concepts of the topic. 1 2 3 4

2. The research task indicates creative thinking. 1 2 3 4

3. The research task is well organised. 1 2 3 4

4. The research task shows substantial research and preparation, using multiple reference sources. 1 2 3 4

5. The research task shows careful use of correct spelling and grammar. 1 2 3 4

6. The oral presentation shows correct pronunciation and clear enunciation. 1 2 3 4

7. The oral presentation shows facial expressions, body movements and eye contact effective in conveying meaning. 1 2 3 4

Teacher comments:

Student comments:

Parent comments:

EXAMPLE: INDIVIDUAL RESEARCH TASK SELF-ASSESSMENT FORM

Name: _____

Task: _____

1 Experiencing difficulty
2 Developing
3 Competent
4 Highly developed

Content:

1. My task was creative and original.	1	2	3	4
2. I used my class time effectively.	1	2	3	4
3. I completed the task.	1	2	3	4
4. I was able to work independently on my task.	1	2	3	4
5. I achieved the outcomes for my task.	1	2	3	4

Comments:

EXAMPLE: GROUP RESEARCH TASK SELF-ASSESSMENT FORM

Names: _____

Task: _____

1 Experiencing difficulty
2 Developing
3 Competent
4 Highly developed

Content:

1. All group members participated.	1	2	3	4
2. The group completed the task.	1	2	3	4
3. The group answered the questions posed by the task.	1	2	3	4
4. The group cooperated on the task.	1	2	3	4

Comments:

EXAMPLE: STUDENT POST-UNIT EVALUATION FORM

Name: _____

1. What new things did you learn by participating in this unit?

2. Were there any parts of the unit that you found repetitive?

3. What did you find the most interesting in this unit? Why?

4. What parts of the unit didn't you enjoy? Why?

5. What activities did you find the most effective for your learning? Why?

6. If you were able to participate in this unit again, what is the most important change you would like to see?

Any other comments?

■ CHAPTER 11

EXAMPLE: TEACHER POST-UNIT EVALUATION FORM

Unit name: _____

1. What appeared to be the major benefits to students from the unit?

2. What activities did they find most motivating?

3. What strategies worked the best in implementing the unit?

4. What aspects of the unit were the most enjoyable to teach? Why?

5. What aspects of the unit didn't work? Why?

6. Would you make any changes to the unit for next time?

Any other comments?

EXAMPLE: TEACHER POST-UNIT EVALUATION FORM

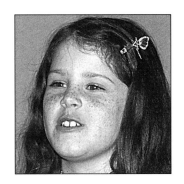

CHAPTER 12
PUTTING IT ALL TOGETHER: EXAMPLES OF UNITS OF WORK

'OUR CHANGING PLANET'

A note from the teacher ...
This unit was designed for a mixed-ability Year 5 or 6 class. The unit provides tasks for individual, small group and whole-class learning using a variety of multidisciplinary activities.

The unit is based on the premise that teachers will have pretested their students to assess their prior knowledge and skills before commencement of the unit tasks. To achieve maximum benefit for gifted students, it is recommended that students be grouped according to academic ability, as much as possible. This will allow like-minded peers to interact at a pace and level appropriate to their academic and socio-affective needs.

It is expected that students participating in this unit will have had some exposure to poetry as a genre, written exposition and debating.

■ CHAPTER 12

RATIONALE

Since its beginning, the world has been constantly changing. Humankind's presence on the timeline of this change has been both comparatively recent and short in duration. However, the effect of this presence has dramatically altered the previously natural progression of this planet.

The primary purpose of this unit is to study the changes that have occurred and are still occurring to our planet, both physically and environmentally. By investigating humankind's effects on these elements, students can evaluate human intervention and predict future possibilities.

This is a multidisciplinary unit that is underpinned by the development of critical and creative thinking skills. Students are encouraged to become active learners by completing a wide range of activities both in class, group and individual structures.

Through the provision of opportunities to interact with their intellectual peers, gifted students will be encouraged to develop their abilities in the higher-order thinking skills of analysis, synthesis and evaluation by working at a faster pace of cognitive reasoning.

DIFFERENTIATION

This unit is designed for students in Years 5 or 6. It differentiates the curriculum for gifted students in the areas of content, process, product and learning environment, according to the principles of Maker. The six strategies for differentiating the curriculum, proposed by Bloom, will form the basis for the unit, while strategies from the model designed by Williams will also be incorporated.

Content

The content of this unit allows gifted students within the class to work on material requiring higher levels of abstraction and complexity.

Process

The unit is designed to be student-centred with the teacher as facilitator for discussions and research. Students will be required to develop their abilities in some of the higher-order thinking processes. The unit includes a strong focus on creative thinking, group problem solving and divergent thinking resulting from open-ended questions.

Product

It is expected that students will demonstrate their abilities to produce creative projects that exemplify the growth of their higher-order thinking skills. Students are able to select from a wide variety of products, both written and oral, to present their individual and group tasks. This will allow products to be consistent with each student's preferred learning style. Opportunities are provided for short-term and long-term independent study projects, depending on student ability.

Learning environment

An environment highlighting openness and a willing acceptance of new ideas and creative thinking will be essential. A student-centred environment, encouraging inquiry and independence, and a wide variety of source materials is necessary for optimal learning.

The activities in this unit may be divided into three sections:

1. **Class activities.** The core lessons are to involve *all* members of the class. These lessons comprise whole-class discussions, group work and individual work, and each is based on Bloom's taxonomy.

2. **Group tasks.** There are opportunities for the completion of differentiated group tasks.

3. **Individual tasks.** These tasks have been designed to allow for varying aptitudes within a class, students' different learning styles, and an element of choice.

UNIT OUTCOMES

Note. The following key will be used to indicate the NSW Board of Studies syllabus from which particular outcomes in this unit have been adapted:

Syllabus:	Key:
'Beyond Stage 3 Outcomes' in the English syllabus, 1998	(English)
'Stage 3 Outcomes' in the HSIE syllabus, 1998	(HSIE)
'Stage 3 Outcomes' in the Science and Technology syllabus, 1999	(Science)

As a result of this unit, students will be able to:

Content:
- demonstrate an understanding of the various forms of written and oral communication, including the purposes and effects of each;
- develop and express sensitivity to language and an awareness of how words, figurative expressions and sentence patterns contribute to the quality of literature;
- apply skills of scientific investigation to group and individual tasks;
- develop mapping, graphing and research skills in order to compile and analyse data;
- incorporate a case study to explore changes that have occurred in environmental areas; (HSIE)
- identify, describe and evaluate the effects of humans on the environment. (Science)

Process:
- use language as a tool for research and communication;
- use discussion to collaborate and negotiate with others when exploring ideas, solving problems, justifying opinions and developing arguments; (English)
- produce a range of texts by selecting aspects and combinations of texts for different purposes and different audience; (English)
- develop and use relevant criteria for assessing the effectiveness of different texts; (English)
- participate in activities that contribute to environmental sustainability; (HSIE)
- make inferences, draw conclusions, and make generalisations about the relationships between people's ways of life and their environment;
- conduct and evaluate their own investigations by observing, questioning, planning, predicting, testing, collecting and recording data and drawing conclusions. (Science)

Product:
- develop products which illustrate their understanding of the structure, style and meaning of various literary genres;
- develop products which reflect their understanding of how to report and interpret findings;
- develop clarity, accuracy and precision in the communication of their understanding;
- select forms of communication appropriate to the purposes and the intended audience; (English)

Learning environment:
- actively seek clarification and expansion of views on ethical issues through open-ended discussions;
- develop a sense of self-worth, responsibility and sensitivity to others through the study of how human beings relate to their physical world;
- develop a set of positive values and attitudes, such as respect for facts, open-mindedness and acceptance of varying points of view;
- demonstrate growth in their desire and ability to seek solutions to environmental problems, both as leaders and as active followers;
- develop skills to evaluate possible resolutions to environmental issues; (HSIE)
- initiate and persevere with investigations. (Science)

CONTENT OUTLINE

A. English:
  1. Accessing text: fiction and nonfiction
  2. Response to literature
  3. Creative writing: poetry and narrative; drama script
  4. Talking and listening: debate and prepared speech
  5. Exposition: letter writing; essays

B. Science and technology:
  1. Geological timeline
  2. Basics of palaeontology
  3. Experiments in plate tectonics
  4. Aquatic field study
  5. Current health issues linked to global warming (links to PD, PE & Health)

C. HSIE:
  1. Patterns of human involvement
  2. Environment: natural patterns of change — affects and response
  3. Case study

D. Creative and practical arts:
  1. Drama: utilisation of dramatic element in group presentation
  2. Music: use of music to portray environmental themes
  3. Dance: utilise dance element in group presentation; use of dance to portray environmental themes
  4. Visual Arts: painting; sketching; sculpture; mural; models; printing

UNIT ACTIVITIES

Science and technology

Whole class

- Investigate the geological timeline with specific reference to its connection to the Australian continent. Create timeline around the classroom based on a scale devised by the students. (Application)
- Investigate Australian flora and fauna of each time period. Employ art skills to represent these on the class timeline. (Application and Synthesis)
- What is palaeontology? (See definition below.) Use a variety of multimedia sources to investigate the science of palaeontology and devise a class definition based on this research. (See Web site references below.) Set up a palaeontology corner in the classroom for students to display typical tools and examples of this science. (Knowledge, Comprehension and Synthesis)

> **A definition of palaeontology**
> Palaeontology is the study of ancient life. The term comes from the old Greek words *palaios*, which means ancient, and *logos*, which means word, or reasoning. Much of our knowledge of the ancient world comes from our study of fossils. Fossils are the remains of ancient plant and animals or the traces of their activities. Bones, shells and teeth are the best-known fossils. But many others, from footprints to fossil dung to minuscule seeds, may be found. Scientists do not only seek the new, the strange or the biggest. They increasingly search for clues to past environments, animal behaviour, and evolution. The smallest fossils may hold the most important clues. Invertebrate palaeontology is the study of animals without backbones, including clams, snails and ammonites. Vertebrate palaeontology is the study of dinosaurs as well as many other types of ancient backboned animals. Palynology is the study of fossil spores and pollens. Sedimentology is the study of the rocks that contain fossils. It provides us with an understanding of ancient physical environments.
> (W. Hortensius, Royal Tyrrell Museum Cooperating Society. 1995 Calgary, Alberta, Canada)

Web sites: Palaeontology
Australian Palaeontology
    URL: http://www.ozemail.com.au/~promote1/auspalaeo/index.html
Australian Museum Online Feature: The Collection — Palaeontology
    URL: http://www.austmus.gov.au/collections/fossils.htm
Research from the Monash University Palaeolab: 'Dinosaur Dreaming'
    URL: http://www.earth.monash.edu.au/dinodream/
Royal Tyrrell Museum: Where Palaeontology Comes Alive!
    URL: http://tyrrellmuseum.com/
University of California, Berkeley. Museum of Palaeontology
    URL: http://www.ucmp.berkeley.edu/

Group tasks
- Experiments in plate tectonics. (See Web site references below.)
- Local field study; temperature, sediment; invertebrate count and identification; identification of native and introduced species of flora. Additional activities: pH tests; turbidity; artificial bromeliad; rainfall gauges; current speed. (The Jason Project, at http://www.jasonproject.org, is a great site to find out how to do these experiments.)
- Debate: 'That Australia needs its feral plants and animals'.

Web sites: Plate Tectonics
Plate Tectonics and People
  URL: http://www.whyallahs.nexus.edu.au/geology/tectonics.htm
Plate Tectonics – The Overall Picture
  URL: http://www.jcu.edu.au/~glpww/EA1001/Plate_Tectonics/Lectures/Causes_of_Plate_Tectonics.html
Earth's Interior and Plate Tectonics
  URL: http://www.anu.edu.au/Physics/solarsystem/eng/earthint.htm
The Ground Beneath – ThinkQuest
  URL: http://library.thinkquest.org/27026/pltect1.htm
This Dynamic Earth: The Story of Plate Tectonics
  URL: http://pubs.usgs.gov/publications/text/dynamic.html
Plate Tectonics (includes lessons for a variety of grade levels)
  URL: http://volcano.und.nodak.edu/vwdocs/vwlessons/plate_tectonics/introduction.html

Individual tasks
- Imagine you are a palaeontologist who has been called on an urgent foreign assignment. What would you pack in your one overnight bag? Justify each item's inclusion. (Synthesis and Evaluation)
- Global warming continues to be a growing concern for scientists and health workers around the world. Investigate one major health issue that has arisen from this problem and present some of the research findings or solutions which are currently being implemented to combat this issue. (Application and Analysis)
- What would happen in Australia if the temperature of the Earth rose 10 degrees Celsius? (Tolerance for ambiguity and Evaluation)
- Evaluate how well the Latin names for the geological time periods suit the characteristics of that period. (Complexity and Evaluation)

HSIE

Whole-class activities
- Identify an environmental issue within your school or local area in need of restorative care and improvement — bush regeneration, litter, waterways, school 'greening', for example. Evaluate a variety of ways of addressing these problems. Design an action plan to present to the school principal and parent body, or to your local government authority, which could be undertaken once approved. (Analysis, Synthesis and Evaluation)

Group tasks
The environment can be affected by both natural and human-induced disasters. Investigate one type of environmental disaster from the following list: bushfire, flood, cyclone, earthquake, drought and plague.

- Research when, where and how disasters of this type have occurred in the Australian environment. (Knowledge, Comprehension and Skills of search)
- Explore one recent example of such a disaster. Use a map to show the location of the area affected by this disaster. Discuss how people and the environment were affected by this disaster. Could this disaster have been prevented? How did people work with nature to help restore the environment after this disaster? (Analysis and Organised random search)
- Explain some ways in which Aboriginal peoples may have coped with and/or utilised such a disaster. (Analysis and Skills of search)
- Write a proposal of at least 500 words suggesting strategies to minimise the impact of a similar disaster in the future. (Synthesis and Examples of change)
- Prepare a presentation of at least five minutes to the class to communicate your findings. This should include one or more elements of music, dance or drama, as well as the use of technology to enhance your presentation. (Synthesis and Visualisation)

Individual task
- Following your local field study, predict how this environment will be different in 50 years time. How could you ensure that any changes to this environment would be beneficial both to the local area itself and to the human use of this area? (Analysis and Evaluation)

Creative and practical arts

Whole class
- Using a variety of media such as paint, pastel and collage materials, create two or three-dimensional examples of the flora and fauna appropriate to each period of the geological timeline to be added to the class wall presentation. (Application and Synthesis)

Group task
- Use dance, music and drama to enhance your group's presentation of their chosen HSIE task. You may wish to use music already available or compose your own melodies and lyrics appropriate to the topic. (Application and Synthesis)

Individual task
- Create an A3 poster to inform, educate, motivate or warn the general public about an Australian environmental issue. The poster should use no more than five words of text. The poster may be created using computer technology or by hand, however a variety of media may be also be effective. Maintain a process journal to indicate your design thoughts and ideas throughout the poster's construction. (Synthesis and Evaluation)

English

Suggested fiction reading
Most of the books in the following list deal with environmental issues.

Author	Title
Laurine Croasdale	*Red Golf Balls*
Jackie French	*House of a Hundred Animals*
	The Metal Men
	The Boy Who Had Wings
	The Music from the Sea
	City in the Sand

Victor Kelleher	*Where the Whales Sing*
Jen McVeity	*Where are the Billabongs?*
James Moloney	*A Bridge to Wiseman's Cove*
Ivan Southall	*Hills End*
	Ash Road
	To the Wild Sky
Theodore Taylor	*The Cay*
Colin Thiele	*Fire in the Stone*
	Martin's Mountain
	Aftershock
	Brahminy: The Story of a Boy and a Sea Eagle
	High Valley
Jules Verne	*Journey to the Center of the Earth*
Yvonne Winer	*Nanangka*

Database activity

Maintain a written or electronic database of the books that you read from the book list. You should cover a minimum of five different authors' works. The following headings should help you construct this:

1. Title of book
2. Author
3. Date published
4. Publisher
5. Genre
6. Protagonist
7. Antagonist
8. Setting
9. Other main characters
10. Plot outline
11. Theme
12. Central conflict
13. Point of view (From whose or which perspective is the story written?)

Whole class

Choose a core reading text from the list to be read by all students based on student ability and text availability.

- Discuss the overall plot and major events of the book. Create a class timeline that differentiates major and minor events in the book. This could be in the form of an event graph or pictorial timeline. (Analysis, Synthesis and Evaluation)
- As a class, compare the relative strengths and weaknesses of the main protagonist and antagonist of the story. This could be recorded as a 'Plus, Minus and Interesting' (PMI) chart (de Bono, 1992) or a simple butcher's paper list. (Analysis)
- Discuss the ways in which the book could be written as a movie script. This discussion should compare and contrast the main elements of script writing with those of narrative writing. For example, are scriptwriters also novelists? Can a script contain the entire text of a novel? Can a scriptwriter alter the novel in any way? How does the scriptwriter show conversation, setting, etc? Then, divide the class into groups to take a small section of the story and write a dramatic script to be performed by members of the class. (Analysis, Synthesis and Creative writing skills)

Group task
- Create a biography board, a multimedia program or a Web page about one of the authors from the list. This presentation should include personal background material about the author; books written and the genre involved; illustrations, graphics, scanned or digitised images; a 'bio-riddle' about the author; a timeline of important events in the author's life and connected historical events; and, in the case of a Web page, any links to related sites should also be utilised. (Organised random search, Study creative process, Visualisation and Synthesis)

Individual tasks
Complete at least two of these activities using books you have read from the above list.
- Write two articles for a newspaper published at the time of a major event in a book. (Application and Creative writing skills)
- Write an interview with one of the protagonists. Record or enact this interview with another member of the class acting as the interviewer. (Application, Synthesis and Intuitive expression)
- Compare the book with several television shows which have similar plots and themes. (Analysis)
- Find three songs that seem to relate to a novel you have read from the list. Write out the lyrics and then create an explanation of how they relate to the book. (Analysis and Evaluation)
- Write an obituary for one of the characters of the book. (Synthesis, Evaluation and Creative writing skills)
- Write an ode to the protagonist of the book. (Synthesis, Evaluation and Creative writing skills)
- Describe an experience you have had that was similar to an experience of a character in the book. (Analysis and Analogy)

■ CHAPTER 12

EXAMPLE: PEER EVALUATION FORM
DEBATE

Name: _____

Peer evaluation of each debate. Use the following scale to evaluate the debate:

1 Not well at all
2 Not very well
3 Moderately well
4 Well
5 Extremely well

1. How well did the first speaker of the team follow the standard rules for a first speaker in a debate?

    5   4   3   2   1

2. How well did the second speaker of the team follow the standard rules for a second speaker in a debate?

    5   4   3   2   1

3. How well did the third speaker of the team follow the standard rules for a third speaker in a debate?

    5   4   3   2   1

4. How well did the team work on rebuttal when listening to the opposing team's speakers?

    5   4   3   2   1

5. How well did the speakers deliver a logical argument?

    5   4   3   2   1

6. Were enlightening conclusions reached by the end of the debate?   Yes / No
    Justify your evaluation:

EXAMPLE: ACTIVITIES
ENGLISH AND TECHNOLOGY UNIT — STAGE 3 (YEAR 6)
'SCIENCE FICTION, FUTURE REALITY?'

Special note. This unit is based on an Internet unit developed by Deborah Gaulin in the Schools of California Online Resources for Educators (SCORE) Project which can be located at http://www.sdcoe.k12.ca.us/score/lengle/lengletg.html. Deborah has kindly given permission for her work to be modified for the purpose of this book.

Teachers' note. This unit is designed to be taught over a term of eight weeks minimum length. Students should be placed in small groups to work on books by one specific author, although they should be encouraged to read from the other lists as well. Students will need time to research each author's Web sites and read four of his or her books. During the reading time they should be working on the biographical sketch research and creating the databases. It is important that, as a facilitator of your students' learning, you have read *at least* one novel by each of the five main authors, so as to be able to gauge relative difficulty levels and appropriate content for each group.

Objectives
During this unit, students will:
- compare and contrast two novels by the same author;
- complete a biographical sketch or 'bio-board' of that author;
- respond to literature using interpretative, critical and evaluative processes;
- create a Web site to share: the 'compare and contrast' essays about the novels written by students in the class, their biographical sketches of their chosen author, and databases of their chosen author's works;
- compare the authenticity of the science fiction issues found in fictional texts with that of print and visual media.

Implementation overview

Description of materials, activities and Web sites
For this unit the teacher will need:
- several copies of the selected authors' novels actually in the classroom, or the novels available in the school library;
- a word-processing program;
- an HTML editor;
- a Web browser and access to the Internet;
- construction paper and art supplies;
- an instruction sheet for a biography board.

Web sites: Sylvia Engdahl
Sylvia Engdahl's Homepage
    URL: http://www.sylviaengdahl.com
Biography
    URL: http://www.angelfire.com/biz/MeishaMerlin/biosylvia.html
Interview with Sylvia Engdahl
    URL:http://www.amazon.com/exec/obidos/show_interview/
    e-s-ngdahlylvialouise/102-0229422-8655309
Distant Star - Sylvia Engdahl
    URL: http://www.distant-star.com/issue10/june_99_engdahl.htm
The Alan Review - Sylvia Engdahl
    URL: http://scholar.lib.vt.edu/ejournals/ALAN/fall97/littlejohn.html
Aslan's Kin - Sylvia Engdahl
    URL: http://www.greenbelt.com/news/aslan/engdahl.htm

■ CHAPTER 12

Web sites: Monica Hughes
Literature by Alberta Authors: Monica Hughes
    URL: http://www.macabees.ab.ca/hughes.html
Monica Hughes - The Promise
    URL: http://www.umanitoba.ca/cm/cmarchive/vol18no3/promise.html
Monica Hughes - The Crystal Drop
    URL: http://www.umanitoba.ca/cm/cmarchive/vol20no2/revcrystaldrop.html
Monica Hughes
    URL: http:www.publib.saskatoon.sk.ca/novel/author/pages/77.html
Young Alberta Book Society: Monica Hughes
    URL: http://www.yabs.ab.ca/hughesm.html
Monica Hughes
    URL: http://www.ecn.ab.ca/mhughes/
Monica Hughes
    URL: http://www.writersunion.ca/h/hughes.htm

Web sites: Madeleine L'Engle
Madeleine L'Engle
    URL: http://wwwvms.utexas.edu/~eithlan/lengle.html
Madeleine L'Engle: Faith During Adversity
    URL: http://www.frugalfun.com/l'engle.html
Madeleine L'Engle Page
    URL: http://www.randomhouse.com/teachers/authors/leng.html
Flying Dreams: Madeleine L'Engle Page
    URL: http://www.mindspring.com/~jlyoung/lengle.htm
Madeleine L'Engle Speech
    URL: http://gos.sbc.edu/l/lengle.html
Madeleine L'Engle Papers
    URL: http://www.lib.usm.edu/~degrum/findaids/l'engle.htm
Biography
    URL: http://www.davison.k12.mi.us/dms/projects/women/alengle.htm
Additional sites:
    URL: http://www.amazon.com/exec/obidos/ts/feature/6238/102-0229422-8655309
    URL: http://www.geocities.com/Athens/Acropolis/8838/
    URL: http://hometown.aol.com/kfbofpql/LEngl.html
    URL: http://www.lunaea.com/words/lengle

Web sites: John Marsden
John Marsden - Darkness, Be My Friend
    URL: http://www.bookworm.com.au/pm001725.htm
John Marsden - The Third Day, The Frost
    URL: http://www.bookworm.com.au/pm001743.htm
John Marsden - The Third Day, The Frost
    URL: http://www.bookworm.com.au/pm001437.htm
John Marsden
    URL: http://www.ozemail.com.au/~andrewf/john.html
John Marsden - The Dead of the Night
    URL: http://www.bookworm.com.au/pm001666.htm
John Marsden
    URL: http://www1.octa4.net.au/jocol/Authors/authorsM.html#marsden
    URL: http://www.sfsite.com/isfdb-bin/exact_author.cgi?John_Marsden
    URL: http://www.noblenet.org/wakefield/zramarsden.htm

Web sites: Gillian Rubenstein
Beaconsfield Primary School - Beacy Book Club
   URL: http://www.beacy.wa.edu.au/library/Beacybookclub.htm
Achuka Interview with Gillian Rubenstein
   URL: http://wwwl.octa4.net.au/jocol/Authors/authorsR.html

Students complete the following activities, using the given Web sites and any others that the students may find in their Internet searches.

Note. These activities are suitable for each of the authors.

Activity 1
Students will gather biographical information, to complete a biographical sketch or a biography board about the chosen author.

Activity 2
Students will use Web sites to create a database of their chosen author's novels and articles.

Activity 3
Students will choose two books written by their author and compare and contrast the texts. It is important to encourage the students within each group to compare different books.

Activity 4
Students will compare issues of science raised in the novels with those they have read in newspapers, magazines or other print media, and/or in television shows and films. They will explain the similarities and differences between the fictional and nonfictional examples.

Activity 5
Working cooperatively in their groups, the students will use the information found in previous activities to create a Web page dedicated to their chosen author.

Assessment
Rubrics are often a helpful way to assess student work, and may be used by the students themselves or by the teacher. The categories of the rubric should be designed around the existing assessment system of the school but the following ideas may be used as a guide.

A key, like the example below, should be provided to explain the rubric.

Key:
0 = no understanding or mastery evident
1 = experiencing difficulty mastering the skill/content
2 = developing mastery of the skill/content
3 = competent mastery of the skill/content
4 = highly developed mastery of the skill/content

EXAMPLE: ASSESSMENT
BIOGRAPHY (BIOGRAPHICAL SKETCH/'BIO-BOARD')

Note. Similar rubrics may be designed for each activity using the current syllabus and outcome documents.

A biography shares the life, thoughts, dreams and achievements of a particular person through the eyes of the author. A biography may be written from the viewpoint which explores the relationship between the author and the subject of the work.

Indicators by which to gauge achievement of outcomes (taken from the 'Stage 3 Outcomes and Indicators' in the NSW Board of Studies English K–6 Syllabus, 1998):

- Extracts information from a media or written text
- Selects resources using skimming techniques, and scans selected texts to locate information
- Writes detailed descriptions
- Uses a variety of print and script styles for effect
- Uses computer software programs and associated hardware to format a variety of texts
- Knows when to change the level of formality in writing
- Uses complex sentences to develop arguments
- Writes sustained arguments and discussions which are supported by evidence
- States different positions about issues
- Writes paragraphs that contain a main idea and elaboration of the main idea

Introduction to students

Your reading tasks in this unit are based on science fiction. The following list will get you started with reading. Many of the books are in trilogies or series so numbers are used to indicate their position in the series. Keep your eye out for newspaper and magazine articles concerning unexplained occurrences and space exploration — you will need all the clues and all the help you can get to discover the key to whether, in fact, science fiction is really our future reality.

Group 1
Sylvia Louise Engdahl
This Star Shall Abide
Enchantress from the Stars
The Far Side of Evil
Beyond the Tomorrow Mountains
The Doors of the Universe
Journey Between Worlds

Group 2
Monica Hughes
The Keeper of the Isis Light (1)
The Guardian of Isis (2)
The Isis Pedlar (3)
The Devil on My Back
The Dream Catcher
Invitation to the Game
Ring-Rise Ring-Set

Group 3
Madeleine L'Engle
A *Wrinkle in Time (1)*
A *Wind in the Door (2)*
A *Swiftly Tilting Planet (3)*
Many Waters (4)
These books are collectively known as the *Time Quartet*.

Group 4

John Marsden	*Tomorrow When the World Began (1)*
	The Dead of the Night (2)
	The Third Day, The Frost (3)
	Darkness, Be My Friend (4)
	Out of Time (5)
	Burning for Revenge (6)
	The Other Side of Dawn (7)

Group 5

Gillian Rubinstein	*Space Demons*
	Galax-Arena
	Skymaze
	Shinkei

Additional reading for avid readers

Note. Some of these books may contain sensitive themes and issues.

Margaret J. Anderson	*In the Circle of Time (1)*
	In the Keep of Time (2)
	The Mists of Time (3)
Damien Broderick and Rory Barnes	*Zones*
Claire Carmichael	*Originator*
	Fabricant
Brian Caswell	*Deucalion*
	The View from Ararat
John Christopher	*The White Mountains (1)*
	The City of Gold and Lead (2)
	The Pool of Fire (3)
Alison Goodman	*Singing the Dogstar Blues*
Virginia Hamilton	*Dustland (2)*
	The Gathering (3)
	Justice and Her Brothers (1)
Catherine Jinks	*Eye to Eye*
Victor Kelleher	*Parkland*
	Earthsong
	Fire Dancer
Robin Klein	*Halfway Across the Galaxy and Turn Right*
	Turn Right for Zyrgon
	Seeing Things
David Luckett	*Night Hunters*
Garth Nix	*Shade's Children*
John O'Brien	*Half Life*
Sally Rogers-Davidson	*Spare Parts*

The following pages are an example of a student instruction sheet for one of the authors on the reading list. This may be adjusted for each author or for the specific needs of the students engaging in this unit.

■ CHAPTER 12

EXAMPLE: STUDENT INSTRUCTION SHEET
AUTHOR STUDY: JOHN MARSDEN

Note. Read through all of the activities before beginning Activity 1. You will need to start reading for Activity 3 immediately.

Activity 1
You will be researching the author John Marsden, creating a biography board or writing a biographical sketch about him.

Task
Using the Internet, find as much information about John Marsden as you can. Then, use the information to create a biography board or biography sketch, utilising computer technology in either biography presentation.

Process
Explore the sites below to find out about John Marsden. Make sure to include in your biography board as many of the following points as you can find:
- Date and place of birth
- Education
- First book written, genre of literature written throughout career so far
- Family background, current family, etc.
- Philosophy of life, ideas and dreams
- Interesting facts

In addition, include your response to the following: Evaluate John Marsden's contribution to the genre of science fiction.
    URL: http://www.ozemail.com.au/~andrewf/john.htm
    URL: http://www.www.sfsite.com/isfdb-bin/exact_author.cgi?John_Marsden
    URL: http://www.noblenet.org/wakefield/zramarsden.htm

Activity 2
Databases are excellent ways to organise information. To help you organise the important aspects of the works of John Marsden, you'll be creating an electronic, annotated database.

Task
Using the Web sites listed below, construct a database of Marsden works.

Process
1. Visit the following sites to get information about the writing of John Marsden:
    Darkness, Be My Friend:
        URL: http://www.bookworm.com.au/pm001725.htm
    The Third Day, The Frost:
        URL: http://www.bookworm.com.au/pm001743.htm
        URL: http://www.bookworm.com.au/pm001437.htm
        URL: http://www.ozemail.com.au/~andrewf/john.html
    The Dead of the Night:
        URL: http://www.bookworm.com.au/pm001666.htm

John Marsden:
>URL: http://www1.octa4.net.au/jocol/Authors/authorsM.html#marsden
>URL: http://www.sfsite.com/isfdb-bin/exact_author.cgi?John_Marsden
>URL: http://www.noblenet.org/wakefield/zramarsden.htm

2. Based on the information from the Internet, construct a database which includes the following information:
   - Name of book
   - Date written
   - Date published
   - Publisher
   - Genre
   - Synopsis
   - Brief critical review of the novel

3. List in the database information on at least four John Marsden books.

Activity 3

You have been researching the author John Marsden. After you have created a biography board or written a biographical sketch about him, and made an annotated database of his works, you can critique two of his works using the following guidelines.

Task

Read two books by John Marsden. Keep a journal as you read, noting down your feelings and reflections about the plot, characters and theme of the novel. After writing a critique of each novel, you will write an essay in which you compare and contrast the novels.

Process

1. Decide which books by John Marsden (from the list) you are going to read.

2. While you are reading, keep a journal.

3. Using your journals, write an essay in which you compare and contrast the two novels you have read.

4. Make sure your essay answers the following questions:
   - How are the characters in each book similar? How are they different?
   - How are the settings similar in each book? How are they different?
   - In what ways are the themes of the books similar? How are they different?
   - What similar literary techniques do you see in the novels?

Activity 4

Make a list of the various issues of a scientific nature that arise in the novels you have read. Compare these to similar scientific issues raised in newspapers, magazines or other print media you are able to source. You may also like to compare them to television and film science documentaries. Explain any similarities and differences between the way these issues are treated in the fictional and nonfictional examples you investigated, presenting your findings in an interesting way.

■ CHAPTER 12

Activity 5

Now that you have: researched John Marsden's background; read four books that he has written; written a response to literature for two books; and researched scientific issues; you are going to make a Web site of your work.

Task

With a group of three other students design a Web page where you can display your essays and link to other sites about John Marsden.

Process

Follow these steps to complete your Web page:

1. Visit the above sites to review the information about John Marsden.

2. Create a Web page dedicated to John Marsden based on the work you have done. The following two Web sites may be of help:
   Creating Web Pages at Jasper High School:
       URL: http://www.sat.net/~vvowel/hyper.html
   Free Art for HTML:
       URL: http://www.mcs.net/~wallach/freeart/buttons.html

CHAPTER 13
MORE SAMPLE ACTIVITIES

he activities on the following pages provide further examples of appropriate tasks for identified gifted students in specific key learning areas. These tasks have been written according to the models of Bloom, Williams, Maker and Kaplan. Where possible, subject, topic and stage are stated. It is not necessary to use all of the tasks, rather, choose a selection which is appropriate to the needs of your class.

EXAMPLE: BLOOM MODEL
ENGLISH — STAGE 2 (YEARS 3 OR 4)
'A SECOND LOOK AT FAIRYTALES'

Application
- What makes a fairytale a fairytale? Make a checklist of requirements a story should satisfy in order to qualify as a fairytale.
- There is an old superstition, that bad things or events happen in threes. Do fairytales reflect this? If so, give some examples.
- Examine the notion of good versus evil in *Little Red Riding Hood*. What parallels can you draw to the present day?
- Rewrite a fairytale of your choice in poetic form.
- Choose one of the characters below. Devise a set of questions you would like to ask the character about his or her role in the story. Interview that character or be the character being interviewed.
  1. The Wolf in *Little Red Riding Hood*
  2. Goldilocks
  3. The Giant in *Jack and the Beanstalk*

Analysis
- Does good have to triumph over evil for a fairytale to work? Examine this question and write your response with references to situations, characters and morals of the tales concerned.
- How many ways could the fairytale you chose have ended? Make a list of these.
- Study four fairytales and try to discover a formula with which they are written.
- Choose one of the following analogies to answer:
  1. How is a fairytale like an instruction manual?
  2. How is a fairytale like a court of law?
  3. How is a fairytale like a political cartoon?
- Compare the role of the royal family in Britain as it is today with that of royal families in fairytales.

Synthesis
- Rewrite one of the fairytales but give each character a different personality. How did this affect the story?
- Write your own fractured fairytale.
- Choose one of the following fairytales and rewrite it as a modern-day story:
  1. *Cinderella*
  2. *The Three Billy Goats Gruff*
  3. *The Three Little Pigs*
- Choose one of the following activities:
  1. Imagine you are Little Red Riding Hood and you realise very quickly that 'Grandma' is actually the Wolf. How will you handle the situation?
  2. Imagine you are Mama Bear and you discover Goldilocks. How will you deal with the situation?
- Choose one fairytale and rewrite it from the point of view of the villain.
- Choose one of the following characters and write about your feelings as if you *were* that character in the event described:
  1. One of the ugly sisters after Cinderella discovers that the shoe fits.
  2. Cinderella when she discovers that the shoe fits.
  3. The Frog Prince sitting on the lily pad.
  4. The Wolf in *The Three Little Pigs* when the third house will not collapse.

5. The Giant in *Jack and the Beanstalk* after Jack steals the goose.
6. The goose that lays the golden egg when Jack arrives to steal her.
- Choose one of the following 'What ifs':
  1. What if Cinderella had been a boy?
  2. What if Jack's mother had not sent Jack to sell the cow?
- How is the advent of fractured fairytales in the late 20th century a symbol of society's changing values?
- Choose one fairytale to consider. Create another character whom the storyteller accidentally left out. What part might that character play in the story? Explain the impact this character might have on the story's progression and on the moral of the story.

Evaluation
- If you characterise fairytales as a conflict between good and evil, with good usually triumphing, how would you characterise fractured fairytales?
- If good is usually triumphant over evil in fairytales, why is the 'bad guy' rarely caught and punished?
- Why do you think fairytales usually have happy endings? Does life reflect this? Explain.
- Explain this analogy: 'Fractured fairytales were to the 20th century what fairytales were to the 19th century'.
- If the characters in fairytales were real people living today, who might they be? Give at least five examples.
- How relevant is the plight of Cinderella's ugly sisters to modern-day society?
- Is society today more a reflection of a traditional fairytale or a fractured fairytale?
- Imagine you are the Wolf from *The Three Little Pigs*. How would you defend your case and convince the judge and jury that you should be found not guilty of the crime against the pigs?

EXAMPLE: MAKER MODEL
SCIENCE — STAGE 1 (YEARS 1 OR 2)
'WEATHER AND OUR SURROUNDINGS'

Content modifications

Abstraction
Meteorologists predict weather for upcoming days. Why is this difficult to do? Write an explanation.

Complexity
Housing styles vary according to the general weather conditions of an area. Research, depict and explain three different styles of housing.

Variety
What is hail? How does it form? Make a model to explain your findings.

Organisation
Using weather temperatures collected over a period of a week, create a graph to record your findings. Were there any noticeable variations? Why?

Study of people
What does a meteorologist do?

Methods of inquiry
You are a teacher planning an excursion to an outdoor venue in summer. What will you need to tell your class to bring? Write a note to tell the parents what to pack for their child for the day.

■ CHAPTER 13

Real problems
The world is becoming warmer (global warming). List some of the problems associated with this and present them to the class. You may choose to focus on one or two problems and present them in greater detail. Explain some of the methods being used to counteract these problems.

Real audiences
Create a play for your class that includes an element of weather surprise, such as a storm, fire, lightning or thunderstorm. Include music and dance in the performance of the play.

Process modifications

Higher-order thinking skills
Analysis
Over a period of a week, study various cloud formations. Draw examples of the different types of clouds you see. Research each type and present your findings in a creative way.

Synthesis
Create a weather station to measure temperature and wind direction. Test it and make suggestions on how to improve your design.

Evaluation
Watch the weather forecasts on television for one week. Note down the predictions and then the weather on the following day. How often was the prediction correct? Why do you think this is so? What is the value of television weather forecasts?

Open-ended processing
Analogy
How is the sun like a light bulb? How is the rain like tears of joy?

Tolerance for ambiguity
What if there were always sunshine and never rain?

Intuitive expression
Changing weather is often associated with different feelings — rain with sadness, for example. Write a poem or paint a picture that depicts your interpretation of a type of weather and the emotion associated with it.

Discovery
Study pictures of satellite imaging that show the progress of a cyclone. Discover how satellite imaging works. Design a visual explanation for your classmates.

Freedom of choice
Choose two adjoining seasons. Create a piece of music using an instrument of your choice to depict the changes in weather between the two seasons.

EXAMPLE: WILLIAMS MODEL
HSIE/SOSE — STAGE 3 (YEARS 5 OR 6)
ANTARCTICA

Paradox
Most people consider that to be blind is to experience only blackness. How is it possible to be blind in a white-out?

Attribute listing
List the 30 most important things you would need on a trip to the Antarctic, OR; Imagine you are playing 'Eye Spy' in Antarctica. List ten things which would make the game challenging but fun.

Analogy
How is the Antarctic like a desert?

Discrepancy

Why is Antarctica a continent when other places, such as Greenland and the Arctic Circle, are not?

Provocative question

Antarctica is rich in minerals? Should we mine it? Write an exposition or discussion.

Examples of change

Research the changes in the use of Antarctica since the beginning of the 1800s. Record your information on a timeline.

Tolerance for ambiguity

What if Scott had made it to the South Pole first?

Skills of search

Set up an experiment to measure the effect of insulation on heat loss. Observe and record your findings. Submit an information report outlining your experiment's results and conclusions.

Intuitive expression

Imagine you are living in one of the huts on an Antarctic base. Write your diary entry or entries. Include some of the following: poetry, lists, sketches, photos, personal insights, jokes, dreams or nightmares.

Adjustment to development

As a civilisation, what have we learned in the past that has meant Antarctica has remained relatively untouched?

Study creative process

Learn about the scientists who are currently studying in the Antarctic. Choose one scientist. Use the Internet to conduct your research and then write an information report that tells about his or her life and work there.

Evaluate situations

Think about what it would be like to take all of the food you would need for a year to live in Antarctica. List ten foods you could and then ten foods you could not live without. Give reasons for each food's inclusion.

Creative reading skills

Read *Journey to Antarctica* by Meredith Hooper. Do you think this journey is the last challenge left in the exploration of this continent?

Creative listening skills

Record a soundtrack of noises that you might hear from your base hut. Use music, sound effects, play your own music, etc.

■ CHAPTER 13

Creative writing skills

'White infinity' is one way of describing the vast, endless ice. There are no natural smells or sounds in the Antarctic (except for the wind). Write a poem to convey the feeling of isolation and 'white infinity'.

Visualisation

Imagine you were able to see the South Pole and the North Pole side by side. What would you see that was similar? What would be different?

EXAMPLE: BLOOM MODEL
SCIENCE AND TECHNOLOGY — STAGE 3 (YEARS 5 OR 6)
'REACH FOR THE STARS'

Application

- How does our Sun compare to other suns? Explain using diagrams, graphs and written descriptions.
- Research the history of American space walks. Develop a timeline that shows each space walk and what was accomplished.
- Construct a two-dimensional plan of a surface space station to be established on the Earth's moon.

Analysis

- Are comets related to meteors or asteroids? Support your opinion with current research.
- Compare and contrast the atmosphere of the Earth and the Moon.
- Research the moons of Saturn and Jupiter. Describe each moon, comparing them to the Earth's moon.

Synthesis

- Write a seven-day diary following the Pathfinder's mission to Mars. Include dates, pictures and factual information.
- Construct a three-dimensional model of a surface space station to be established on Earth's moon. Label each section, including explanations and proposed uses.
- Choose five constellations. Draw the patterns they form and evaluate the names they have been given in relation to these patterns.
- You have been selected by NASA to design a plaque or poster which will be placed on the next deep-space probe. The purpose of the plaque or poster is to let other life forms in the Universe learn about Earth and its inhabitants. You may use any art form, but the plaque or poster must be scientifically correct. You must include an essay with it which explains why you included the items on the plaque or poster. This will be included on a computer chip on the probe to provide a further understanding of our Earth.
- Design a tourist campaign for another planet or galaxy, based on the scientific facts as we know them. The campaign should include advertising in the form of posters and short radio advertisements.

Evaluation

- Evaluate the Voyager travels. Explain how they have changed our perceptions of, and added to our knowledge of, our solar system.
- Should we attempt to contact alien life if we find it? Why or why not?
- Express your opinion of the search for extraterrestrials.

EXAMPLE: BLOOM MODEL
ENGLISH — STAGES 2 AND 3 (YEARS 3 TO 6)
NOVEL STUDIES

Application
- Write any kind of poem (minimum sixteen lines) about your novel, which illustrates an important message of the novel.
- Write an obituary for one character, which would be found in a newspaper in the era of novel's setting.
- Write an interview with the protagonist of the novel. Explore his or her feelings about the key events in the novel.
- Design a board game to be sold with the book which highlights the major events of the plot.

Analysis
- Tell what you think happened before the story began.
- Write a review of a movie that is similar to your novel in plot or in general theme.
- Describe an experience you've had that was similar to the experience of a character in the book.
- Discuss how the main character is like or unlike a person (or animal) you know.
- To what age group does the book appeal? Make a prediction and then design a research study to discover the actual answer.
- Compare the book to another the author has written, or to a book in the same genre by another author. What are the similarities and differences?

Synthesis
- Explain how you would make the book you read into a movie. Who would play the main characters, where would you film it, etc?
- Write two articles for a newspaper published at the time of a major event in your book.
- Create a collage of a major theme in the novel or one which illustrates parts of the novel.
- Find three songs which seem to relate to the novel you read. Write out the lyrics and then write an explanation of how they relate to the novel.
- Write several diary entries made by one of the major characters of the novel.
- Continue the story to describe what happens next.
- Choose a specific curriculum model, such as Bloom or Williams, to use and design a unit of work for your peers based on this novel.

Evaluation
- Explain why you would like to have one of the characters as a friend.
- What is the theme of the novel? How effectively do you believe the author has conveyed this message?
- Imagine you are one of the main characters of the novel. What suggestions would you make to the author for improving and/or changing your part in the story?
- A character from the story has been put on trial. Choose to be a lawyer to defend or to prosecute this character and build your case. (Extension: Find another student who has taken the opposing viewpoint and conduct a 'mock' trial.)
- Should this novel be required reading for all students at Stages 2 and 3? Why or why not?

■ CHAPTER 13

EXAMPLE: BLOOM MODEL
ENGLISH — STAGE 3 (YEARS 5 OR 6)
A CAGE OF BUTTERFLIES **BY BRIAN CASWELL**

Analysis
What do you think the farm is? What pictures come to mind when you think of the farm? Do you think places like the farm exist in real life?

Application
Design a story web to chart the different events in the story.

Evaluation
Larsen and Susan have different opinions about the way things are done at the farm. How are their ideas alike? How are they different? What are your opinions about the treatment of the children at the farm? Include specific examples to support your views.

Analysis and Synthesis
The twins communicate differently to other people. Explain this communication. Have you ever felt communication between you and someone else that has not needed words? Describe.

Synthesis and Evaluation
Do you think communication such as that used by the twins is possible? Support your views with examples. You may like to use the Internet to discover recent research in this field of psychology.

Analysis
Does the novel's prologue give you any clues as to the plot and/or theme of the novel? Compare and contrast the prologue to a recent movie trailer you may have seen.

Evaluation
What is the theme of this novel? Discuss how you feel this theme relates to your life. Should all students in your year read this novel? Why or why not?

EXAMPLE: WILLIAMS MODEL
SCIENCE AND TECHNOLOGY — STAGE 3 (YEARS 5 OR 6)
INVENTIONS

Paradox
Discuss the statement: 'Necessity is the mother of invention'.

Attribute listing
List the most famous inventors of the 20th century.

Analogy
How is an inventor like a battery?

Discrepancy
Electricity goes off in your house for a week. How does this affect your household and what do you do to cope?

Provocative question
What invention would you not be able to live without? How do your choices compare with those of your peers? Your parents? Other adults?

Examples of change
What inventions of the last decade have changed your way of living? Explain, giving at least two examples. What do you regard as the most important invention or discovery of the past century?

Examples of habit
Study and explain alternative sources of energy to drive machines. Who invented the ideas to utilise these energy sources? Are these energy sources widely used? Why or why not?

Tolerance for ambiguity
What would the world be like if the Wright brothers had not invented their 'flying machine'?

Skills of search
Research the inventions which have received national awards in the last two decades. What were the criteria on which they were judged to receive the award? Did these inventions change our way of life? Why or why not?

Intuitive expression
Design an invention for the year 3000. Write a narrative about the ways your invention is of benefit to humankind.

Adjustment to development
You have just invented a new machine. Follow the process of invention, from idea to manufacture to distribution.

Study creative process
Research the life of Leonardo da Vinci, with specific focus on his role as an inventor. What processes did he undertake to design, test and record his inventions?

Evaluate situations
A new environmental law has recently been passed which restricts all households to the use of only three electrical appliances, aside from electrical lighting. What three machines would you choose and how would you cope without the other machines?

Creative reading skills
Read *Music from the Sea* by Jackie French. What machines do the people of the 'valley' have? What machines are missing? Why is this the case?

Creative listening skills
The Australian group the 'Tap Dogs' perform by tap dancing on everything possible. Most of the performance is without music, using synchronised and syncopated rhythms of the steel-plated shoes to create a percussive effect. Watch the video of one of their performances and write a percussive score for a section of one routine.

EXAMPLE: MAKER MODEL
INTERDISCIPLINARY — STAGE 2 (YEARS 3 OR 4)
CATS

Content modifications

Abstraction
'I wonder why no human ever seems to catch on
That things that aren't forbidden are no fun to scratch on.'
This poem is titled 'Paradox' and the author listed as Ogden Nash's Cat. How true a paradox is it?

Complexity
Compile a list of 'big cats'. What makes each of these 'big cats' different? How are they similar?

Variety
When were cats first domesticated? How has the role of cats changed from that time to the present day?

Organisation
Create a survey to discover the percentage of students in your year who have a cat as a pet. How does this percentage compare to other types of pets? What types of cats do the students have as pets? Why do people choose a cat for a pet?

Study of people
Study the research of one of the scientists or environmentalists who are working, or have worked, with an endangered species.

Methods of inquiry
How do scientists and environmentalists decide what animals should be placed on the endangered species list?

Process modifications

Higher-order thinking skills
Analysis
Feral cats are an increasing problem to the preservation of native wildlife. Compare and contrast different alternatives being used to deal with this issue.
Synthesis
Keep a log for one week of all the times you come into contact with, or see, a cat. Keep a note of the types of cats (real, cartoon, fictional, etc.), the situations in which you encountered them and the emotional responses to these cats by those around them (humour, anger, love, etc.). Find a creative way to show how important cats are to our everyday lives.
Evaluation
You have been asked to recommend a specific breed of cat as a pet for a young child. Decide what information you would need to know to make this recommendation. Choose the three most appropriate cats, giving information about them and your reasons for their inclusion.

Open-ended processing
Paradox
A cat is said to have nine lives. Is this possible? Why or why not?
Analogy
How is a cat like a pincushion?
Tolerance for ambiguity
What if there were no cats, wild or domestic? How would our world be different?
Intuitive expression
Read *Poetry for Cats* by Henry Beard in which many famous poets' verses have been altered to relate to cats. Choose a poem by a poet not featured in this book and create your own 'distinguished feline verse'.
Discovery
There are many sayings in the English language about cats, such as 'cats always land on their feet' and 'curiosity killed the cat', which are used as personifications. Find more of these sayings and discover their origins and original meanings.
Freedom of choice
A number of 'big cats' are on the endangered species list or soon will be. Choose one of these and design an awareness campaign to encourage its protection and preservation for the future.
Group interaction
Conduct a debate: 'That wearing animal furs should be a criminal offence'.

Product modifications

Real world problems
Migration 'corridors' for wild animals are rapidly disappearing due to human population expansion and many species are no longer able to find direct routes to their food sources and breeding areas. What can be done to ensure that this problem is addressed by world governments? Are there any programs under way currently to restore migration 'corridors'?
Real audiences
Domestic cats are a threat to Australian native wildlife. Design an awareness program to alert school children to the problem and encourage those who have pet cats to keep them indoors at night. Present your proposal for this program to the appropriate decision-makers, such as the School Principal, School Executive or School Council.

CHAPTER 14
THE HARRY POTTER SERIES
GROSS

ne of the most commonly noted characteristics of intellectually gifted students is a passionate love for reading. Many gifted students teach themselves to read before they enter school (Gross, 1999). The accelerated reading abilities and reading interests possessed by the majority of intellectually gifted students lead them to choose books which are generally preferred by children of average ability who are several years older.

In the first half of the last century gifted children and adolescents, in studies conducted by Terman (1925), Carroll (1940) and Hollingworth (1942), named as their favourite books many of the traditional 'classics' of literature — the historical novels of Scott, Stevenson and Dumas, for example. Many of these books traced the development of individuals or societies through their pursuit of a 'quest'. This often took the form of an individual's search for identity or personal morality, or a community's quest for identity through nationhood or adherence to a faith.

What types of literature are preferred by the current generations of gifted and talented children? More recent studies (e.g. Kolloff, 1985; Gross, 1993) show that 'quest' novels are still overwhelmingly popular. The period and settings of the newer novels have changed, but the themes are remarkably similar. The *Narnia* chronicles of C. S. Lewis, Tolkien's 'middle-earth' saga, Ursula LeGuin's *Earthsea* series, Madeleine L'Engle's *A Wrinkle in Time* and Isobelle Carmody's *The Gathering* are excellent examples of what Halstead (1988) calls 'high fantasy' — in which the protagonists are drawn into a quest by forces beyond their control, in which they fight against evil or injustice.

The Harry Potter books have fired the imagination of children the world over and, not surprisingly, gifted children appear to be particularly enthralled by them. Children with wide and rich vocabularies particularly enjoy the humour which often involves sophisticated word play, and the invented language of spells derived from Latin. (The *Asterix* series has a similar appeal.) There are countless allusions to Greek and Roman mythology with which many gifted students may already be familiar.

The Harry Potter series is a remarkable contribution to the genre of 'high fantasy' which has been discussed in Chapter 10. Like many other heroes of myth and legend, Harry's origins are at first shrouded in mystery. Over the course of the first book he begins to discover who he is and the role he is fated to play in a fight against evil, which is necessary if the society in which he lives is to survive. He is supported by loyal friends Hermione and Ron, protected, advised and guided by a kindly and powerful sage Albus Dumbledore who is the symbol of wisdom, far-seeing vision and sanity, and opposed by a deadly foe who is the personification of evil, Lord Voldemort. Harry must survive a number of rites of passage in order to develop the knowledge, wisdom, skill and maturity which will enable him to defend his home, Hogwarts, and his friends against Lord Voldemort's loathing and ambition.

In the first book of the series, Harry's personal quest for identity is given prominence over the deeper theme of good versus evil, or dark versus light. As the series progresses, however, the reader becomes aware that Harry's growth towards personal maturity, and towards a system of personal morality, is crucial to the battle between light and darkness which emerges as the dominant theme in the subsequent novels, particularly the third and fourth.

Several themes appear throughout the Harry Potter series which, while they are relevant to and appeal to many children, may have a particular attraction or relevance for intellectually gifted children.

The conflict between good and evil

Researchers studying intellectually gifted children have frequently noted an unusually accelerated development of moral reasoning (Hollingworth, 1942; Silverman, 1993; Gross, 1993). This is often characterised by a passionate concern for justice and fairness, a deep interest in ethical or moral issues, and sometimes an unusually deep and mature interest in questions of origin, destiny and humankind's relationship with God. These children may protest quite vigorously against actions of other students, or even teachers, which they believe violate the principles of honesty or equity.

Children such as these can become passionately involved in the moral issues proposed in the Harry Potter series and may enquire much more deeply into the story than is usual for their age. For example, even in the early years of school, gifted students may note that the Dark Lord's cohorts serve him out of fear, through enchantment (literally) or from a desire for power, while Harry's friends support him out of friendship, loyalty and a conviction that they are fighting against evil.

In media interviews, Joanne Rowling, the author of the Harry Potter series, has responded to critics who say that her books are too dark by saying that she wants to teach children that evil is real and that it is destructive.

Perhaps the darkest and most terrifying creatures in the books are the Dementors, soulless guards of the prison of Azkaban, who feed on human emotions. In *Harry Potter and the Prisoner of Azkaban*, Professor Lupin says of them:

> Dementors are among the foulest creatures that walk this earth. They infest the darkest, filthiest places, they glory in decay and despair, they drain peace, hope and happiness out of the air. Even Muggles feel their presence, although they can't see them. Go too near a Dementor and every good feeling, every happy memory, will be sucked out of you. If it can, the Dementor will feed on you long enough to reduce you to something like itself — soulless and evil. You'll be left with nothing but the worst experiences of your life.
> (*Harry Potter and the Prisoner of Azkaban*, p. 140)

Lupin then points out that the Dementors would have been excited by the high emotions around the Quidditch match: 'I don't think they could resist the large crowd around the Quidditch pitch. All that excitement — emotions running high — it was their idea of a feast'. This may be an allusion to the infectious and destructive qualities of crowd hysteria — people feeding off each other's anger, or mindlessly following a charismatic leader. A dominant theme in the series is the fight against evil, injustice and bigotry. It is notable that many of the key incidents in the series, which Rowling is careful to date, coincide with critical dates from World War II.

Persecution of people who are different

Events throughout the series portray two types of opposition to people who differ from the norm — active and passive opposition. Resentment of people who are 'different' may arise, in part, through a fear of something unknown and strange. Who one views as different depends, of course, on the group to which one belongs!

Three distinct groups inhabit the world of Harry Potter:

1. People of pure wizard ancestry like Harry's schoolfriend Ron
2. People of mixed, wizard and non-wizard, ancestry — Mudbloods like Harry Potter himself
3. People with no wizard ancestry — Muggles like Harry's schoolfriend Hermione

Certain groups within Hogwarts School, particularly Draco Malfoy, his family and his friends in Slytherin House, pursue a policy of active opposition to Mudbloods and Muggles. They are dedicated to keeping people of 'impure' blood out of Hogwarts and out of positions of power in the wizard world. This theme is graphically illustrated in the book through examples of dominant groups tormenting or harassing individuals whom they believe to be 'different' or inferior. In the fourth book, when Lord Voldemort returns to power, Malfoy joyfully predicts increasing danger for Harry, who is a Mudblood. Ironically, the Dursleys who are Muggles, also initially torment and harass Harry because his part-wizard blood makes him different from them.

Passive opposition is the refusal to assist or defend the individual who is being bullied or harassed. Gifted and talented students are frequently mocked, derided and bullied because they are different. Not only these students, but also teachers who wish to develop special programs to assist them, may suffer both active and passive opposition.

Acceleration as an unquestioned response to high natural ability

In the first four books of the series there are four overtly described instances of Harry Potter being accelerated.

In the first book, Harry is found to have a brilliant natural aptitude for sport. He is accelerated — not academically, but specifically within Quidditch, the sport in which he excels. He plays on a school team composed of students who are from one grade to several grades older than him. He is the youngest person in 100 years to play on a Quidditch team.

No great fuss is made over Harry's acceleration. It is simply accepted that he will not be able to develop his gift to the fullest in the company of age-peers, who have not developed to his present level of expertise. This 'subject acceleration' is the school's immediate and logical response.

Can your students find the other three examples?

Problems solved by high intelligence and application

Hermione is of pure Muggle origin. Perhaps because of this, she is initially extremely anxious about her chances of success at Hogwarts and studies relentlessly. This irritates people intensely. However, Rowling emphasises that Hermione is extremely bright and describes her (*Harry Potter and the Prisoner of Azkaban*, p. 9) as the cleverest witch in Harry's year.

In the first book, Hermione is persecuted by the Hogwarts students for being bright and studious. Harry is forgiven for being bright because he is talented at sport and because he does not particularly enjoy studying. This provides a fascinating analogy with research conducted in Australia (Carrington, 1993) and the United States (Tannenbaum, 1962) on adolescent attitudes to gifted students. These studies found that the most socially acceptable students in American and Australian schools were students of average ability who did not study and who were athletically inclined, while the least popular were brilliant students who enjoyed studying and were not athletically inclined.

Hermione is also persecuted by Malfoy and his cronies for being a Muggle. Even some teachers initially resent her. Professor Snape calls her an 'insufferable know-it-all'.

Yet at no time does Hermione use her abilities for evil or, except for one occasion in *Harry Potter and the Goblet of Fire*, in retaliation against people who are unpleasant to her. Indeed, she consistently comes up with the solutions to problems to get Ron and Harry out of trouble. It is Hermione who is trusted, intellectually and emotionally, by Professor McGonagall, to use the spell which will allow her to go back in time and change the course of events. Harry succeeds in the Triwizard Tournament largely because Hermione has trained him in the use of critical spells.

Hermione defies the detractors who suggest that Muggleborn people are not capable of becoming real wizards. She succeeds because she is extremely bright, intellectually resilient and willing to work hard.

Using the Harry Potter series with gifted and talented students

The Harry Potter series may be a useful vehicle to help children to discuss both issues pertinent to the education of gifted and talented students, for example acceleration, the mistrust of people who are different and the search for self and self-acceptance even though one *is* different, and wider issues which should concern all students but which, because of their unusual intellectual and emotional maturity, may awaken the interest and concern of gifted students at somewhat earlier ages than are usual.

The following examples from the Williams, Maker and Bloom/Krathwohl curriculum models are built around the first four books in the Harry Potter series. Each of the first four matrices is designed around a specific book in the series while the fifth covers the series as a whole. As with the other material in this book, the examples are designed to respond to the cognitive and affective needs and characteristics of intellectually gifted students.

TABLE 18
WILLIAMS MODEL MATRIX
ENGLISH — EARLY STAGE 2 (YEARS 2 OR 3)
***HARRY POTTER AND THE PHILOSOPHER'S STONE* BY J. K. ROWLING**

PARADOX	Make a timeline of the events in the book. Pretend you are Harry Potter and rank the events in the story from very sad to very happy. Now pretend you are Draco Malfoy and do the same. How does the order change? Can events be sad and happy at the same time?
ATTRIBUTE LISTING	Many of the people or creatures in this book have names that indicate their jobs, personalities or interests. How many can you find whose names hint at their jobs?
ANALOGY	How is Professor Dumbledore like Aslan in C. S. Lewis' *The Lion, the Witch and the Wardrobe?*
DISCREPANCY	If Neville had not been part of this story, would the story have ended differently?
PROVOCATIVE QUESTION	When Harry Potter looks in the Mirror of Erised he sees his parents. If Draco Malfoy looked in the Mirror, what do you think he would see? If Hermione looked in the Mirror, what do you think she would see?
EXAMPLES OF CHANGE	How does the way Harry and Hermione feel about each other change during the story?
EXAMPLES OF HABIT	Often in fantasy stories good people have fair hair and bad people have dark hair. How does J. K. Rowling change this?
ORGANISED RANDOM SEARCH	The author gives different models of broomsticks different names to suggest how desirable they are. Which broomsticks do you think are least desirable? Which do you think are most desirable and why?
SKILLS OF SEARCH	Look carefully at the names which toy manufacturers give to their toys to make children want to buy them. What do you notice about the names of very popular toys?
TOLERANCE FOR AMBIGUITY	What might have happened if the Dursleys had welcomed Harry Potter into their family and treated him kindly?
INTUITIVE EXPRESSION	You are Draco Malfoy. How do you feel when Harry Potter tells Professor Flitwick that it is thanks to you that he has his wonderful new broomstick?
ADJUSTMENT TO DEVELOPMENT	List the good and bad things that happen to Harry Potter in the first and last chapters of this book. How does the pattern change?
STUDY CREATIVE PROCESS	Sometimes J. K. Rowling likes putting in touches of humour to lighten sad situations. How does she introduce humour to Harry's unhappy treatment by the Dursleys?
EVALUATE SITUATIONS	Generally, in traditional fairy stories, good people are always rewarded and bad people are always punished. Does J. K. Rowling keep to this 'rule'?
CREATIVE READING SKILLS	Read the story from Greek mythology about Charon and his three-headed dog Cerberus. What similarities are there between Cerberus and Hagrid's pet Fluffy?
CREATIVE LISTENING SKILLS	Listen to 'The Hut on Fowl's Legs' from Mussorgsky's *Pictures at an Exhibition*. If you were making a film of *Harry Potter and the Philosopher's Stone*, which scene might you accompany with this music?
CREATIVE WRITING SKILLS	Pretend you are Hedwig the owl. Write a letter to an owl friend telling how Harry chose you. How did you feel when you were chosen?
VISUALISATION	Describe how the Great Hall would have been decorated if Ravenclaw had won the House Cup.

From Gross, MacLeod, Drummond and Merrick (2001) *Gifted Students in Primary Schools: Differentiating the Curriculum* Sydney: GERRIC.

CHAPTER 14

TABLE 19
MAKER MODIFICATIONS MATRIX
ENGLISH — STAGE 2 (YEARS 3 OR 4)
***HARRY POTTER AND THE CHAMBER OF SECRETS* BY J. K. ROWLING**

CONTENT / PROCESS	COMPLEXITY	STUDY OF PEOPLE	VARIETY
ANALYSIS	In the 'real world' we would think someone with magical powers was 'different' but at Hogwarts someone who is not of pure wizard blood is 'different'. How do Draco Malfoy and his friends behave towards people who are different? How do you feel about their behaviour? If you had magical powers, would you want people to know? Why? Why not?	J. K. Rowling describes herself when she was a child as being a rather shy, studious, unathletic girl who wore glasses and earned mostly high grades at school. Which character in the Harry Potter books does this sound like? What strengths and what weaknesses does Rowling give this character?	In the closing chapter, Dumbledore says, 'It is our choices, Harry, that show what we truly are, far more than our abilities'. Do you agree or disagree with this statement? You might use examples from literature, from mythology or from history to defend your argument.
PARADOX	Dobby the elf cries when Harry treats him with kindness. Why do we sometimes cry at happy events? Has this ever happened to you? Create a visual image of what happened, or how you felt.	Many objects in the Harry Potter books are personified — given personalities and feelings. The Weasleys' flying car helps Harry but then abandons him in a crisis. How does the car show its feelings? What might have been some reasons for its contradictory behaviour?	In Harry's duel with the Basilisk, his life is saved by the tears of Fawkes the Phoenix. What other examples can you think of from literature where hardship or grief suffered by one character saves another character from greater hardship?
DISCOVERY	Greek and Roman mythology contains many creatures which have the power to harm humans but which are overcome by the courage and quick-wittedness of a single man or woman. Research some of these creatures. How are their stories similar to events in *Harry Potter and the Chamber of Secrets*?	Harry Potter is probably most people's favourite character in this book. Interview some of your classmates to find out who is their second-favourite character and why. Do they like the character because of his or her personality, or because of the part they play in the story, or because of the way the author describes them, or for some other reason?	Interview three students of different ages who have read *Harry Potter and the Chamber of Secrets*. What did these students think about the book? How did they compare it to the first book in the series? What similarities and differences do you note in their opinions?

From Gross, MacLeod, Drummond and Merrick (2001) *Gifted Students in Primary Schools: Differentiating the Curriculum* Sydney: GERRIC.

CHAPTER 14

TABLE 20
MAKER MODIFICATIONS MATRIX
ENGLISH — STAGE 3 (YEARS 5 OR 6)
***HARRY POTTER AND THE PRISONER OF AZKABAN* BY J. K. ROWLING**

CONTENT PROCESS	METHODS OF INQUIRY	STUDY OF PEOPLE	VARIETY
ANALYSIS	The 'magic words' which Rowling creates for many spells won't be found in a dictionary! However, they are derived from Latin, as are many English words which *are* in the dictionary. Use a dictionary creatively to find the meanings of 'expelliarmus', 'mobilcorpus' and other spells used in this book.	Before J. K. Rowling became a full-time author, she was a teacher of French and Latin. She uses her knowledge of schools and her talents in language to make the Harry Potter books even more effective. If you wanted to become an author what talents and experiences do you have that you could draw on to develop the plots for your stories?	Hagrid's fondness for dangerous creatures regularly gets him into trouble. What dangerous creatures from Greek mythology have we not yet met in the Harry Potter series? Which of them might be an interesting pet for Hagrid and what problems could arise as a result of this?
PARADOX	A werewolf is traditionally a terrifying and evil figure. Yet Lupin was loved so much by his school friends that they took enormous risks to support him. What other deep friendships do you know of in history and literature which survived danger and misunderstanding?	Why, when Harry Potter is the 'hero' of this book, is it Hermione who is trusted with the responsibility of changing time?	The Boggart takes the shape of one's greatest fear but the fear can be banished by confronting it. What might be the greatest fear of some of the 'good' characters in the book — Dumbledore, Hermione and Sirius Black, for example? What about the 'bad' characters like Draco Malfoy, Lucius Malfoy and a Dementor?
DISCOVERY	The Malfoys would like to rid Slytherin House of people who are not of pure wizard blood. Why do they want to do this? How would you feel if you were one of the people they want to remove? Discover an incident in history or in current times where this attitude was held by a group of people. What happened? What was the result of their actions?	In Chapter 19, Sirius Black calls Voldemort 'the biggest bully in the playground'. What is a 'bully'? What characteristics does Voldemort share with bullies? Why does someone become a bully?	Lupin says that the Dementors 'feed off' the emotions generated by the Quidditch match. What situations can you think of where large crowds of people become caught up in each other's feelings? Are there both positive and negative examples of this?

From Gross, MacLeod, Drummond and Merrick (2001) *Gifted Students in Primary Schools: Differentiating the Curriculum* Sydney: GERRIC.

CHAPTER 14

TABLE 21
BLOOM ENRICHMENT MATRIX
ENGLISH — LATE STAGE 3 (YEARS 6 OR 7)
HARRY POTTER AND THE GOBLET OF FIRE BY J. K. ROWLING

CONTENT	APPLICATION	ANALYSIS	SYNTHESIS	EVALUATION
Characterisation	Design a chart which illustrates, chapter by chapter, which characters in this book seem to be 'good', which characters seem to be 'evil' and which seem to have elements of both. Make sure you trace the paths of characters who seem to change categories as the plot progresses.	The Greek philosopher Aristotle said that a true friend feels only happiness when good things happen to his friends. Is Ron a true friend to Harry?	People who predict disaster are often disliked and resented — even when their predictions come true and they are shown to be right. In what ways does 'Mad Eye' Moony resemble the character Cassandra from Greek mythology?	In this book we are given information about Neville and Professor Snape which was withheld from us in previous books. How effectively does this 'new' information explain some of Neville's and Snape's behaviour in earlier books?
Plot construction	Draw or paint a picture, or create a diorama, of an event or situation in the book which is critical to the plot. Can you find a way of showing the feelings, as well as the actions, of the people involved?	What are the principal characteristics of Veelas? How does this influence what happens in the story?	There are several occasions in this book where Harry refuses to accept advantages or opportunities which he considers would be unfair to his opponents. How do his refusals influence further developments in the story?	How effectively does J. K. Rowling use the character of Ludo Bagman to move the plot forward?
Use of symbolism	Dumbledore's Pensieve serves as a symbol of how our thoughts and memories are interconnected. Draw a diagram of the thoughts and memories which must have thronged Harry's mind at the end of this story.	Compare and contrast J. K. Rowling's use of colour in three settings: the Quidditch World Cup Stadium, the Goblet of Fire scenes and the Yule Ball. Do any patterns appear?	When a group of wizards molest a Muggle family in Chapter 9, they wear hoods and masks. Why do they do this? How is this incident similar to a recent event in the media? Can there be a situation when wearing hoods and/or masks can be for a positive reason?	Invisibility cloaks appear in many fairy tales, myths and legends. These cloaks both protect the wearer and give him or her power. To what degree does Harry Potter's invisibility cloak serve both purposes?
Theme	Organise a class debate on the topic: 'Harry Potter could not have survived the Triwizard tournament without the help of Hermione'.	Distinguish events in the story which arise from fear or resentment of people who are 'different'. How do these events influence the course of the plot?	In Chapter 23 Hermione and Ron express contrasting attitudes towards the purpose of the Triwizard Tournament. How does this reflect community attitudes towards other international competitions such as the Olympic Games?	When the masked wizards molest the Muggle family, some other wizards disapprove but do not interfere. Is refusing to fight evil as bad as engaging in it? Explain your opinions, giving examples from literature, history or the media to support your thoughts.

From Gross, MacLeod, Drummond and Merrick (2001) *Gifted Students in Primary Schools: Differentiating the Curriculum* Sydney: GERRIC.

CHAPTER 14

TABLE 22
WILLIAMS MODEL MATRIX
ENGLISH — ABOVE STAGE 3
THE HARRY POTTER SERIES OF BOOKS BY J. K. ROWLING

PARADOX	Towards the end of the first book of the series, Professor Dumbledore says: 'The truth. It is a beautiful and terrible thing and should therefore be treated with great caution'. What truths can you find in the Harry Potter series which are both beautiful and terrible?
ATTRIBUTE LISTING	In *Harry Potter and the Prisoner of Azkaban*, Harry escapes from the angry Dursleys and is rescued by the Knight Bus. In what ways does the bus resemble the knights in the stories of King Arthur?
ANALOGY	How is Hermione like a candle?
DISCREPANCY	Lord Voldemort is portrayed as pure evil. Is there any character in the Harry Potter series who is portrayed as pure goodness?
PROVOCATIVE QUESTION	Why do you think J. K. Rowling portrays the white chessmen in Chapter 16 of *Harry Potter and the Philosopher's Stone* as having no faces?
EXAMPLES OF CHANGE	How do our attitudes to Sirius Black change over the course of *Harry Potter and the Prisoner of Azkaban*?
EXAMPLES OF HABIT	Schools usually expect children of the same age to work together, but even in the first book Harry is accelerated by being allowed to work with older students in Quidditch. Where else in the series is Harry treated as if he were older?
ORGANISED RANDOM SEARCH	Ron Weasley is supportive of Hermione on some occasions but not on others. Are there any patterns in his behaviour?
SKILLS OF SEARCH	Access one of the many Web sites devoted to the Harry Potter books. Choose a critic's evaluation of the Harry Potter series. To what degree do you agree or disagree with the critic's comments?
TOLERANCE FOR AMBIGUITY	How might the plot of the series have changed if Buckbeak had been found innocent?
INTUITIVE EXPRESSION	Listen to Wagner's stirring 'Ride of the Valkyries' from his opera *Die Walküre*. Imagine you are Harry or Hermione riding to Sirius Black's rescue on Buckbeak's back. Create a song you might chant as you ride.
ADJUSTMENT TO DEVELOPMENT	At the start of the series Hermione is resented for being academically talented but Harry is admired because he is talented at Quidditch. Does this bias exist in the real world?
STUDY CREATIVE PROCESS	C. S. Lewis, author of the *Narnia* series, and Madeleine L'Engle, author of *A Wrinkle in Time*, created 'different worlds' of people and ideas rather as J. K. Rowling has done. Read about how any of these three authors developed their ideas. Find a creative way to share your findings.
EVALUATE SITUATIONS	Several dates which appear in the Harry Potter series are actually important dates from World War II. For example, June 6th, the date that Harry and Hermione rescue Sirius Black from the Shrieking Shack, is the date in 1944 when the Allies landed in Normandy to liberate Europe. See if you can find similar matches of dates. What may be J. K. Rowling's intention in this?
CREATIVE READING SKILLS	Read J. R. R. Tolkien's novel *The Hobbit*. How does the central character of Bilbo Baggins resemble Harry Potter and in what ways are they different? Are there any similarities between Gandalf and Professor Dumbledore?
CREATIVE LISTENING SKILLS	Ask three people to describe to you what they feel is the most exciting scene from any of the Harry Potter books. Pretend you are J. K. Rowling and use what you feel are the key elements of their scenes to create a scene which could feature in the fifth book.
CREATIVE WRITING SKILLS	J. K. Rowling gives many of her characters names which illustrate their personality. Create middle names for Harry Potter, Fleur Delacour, Draco Malfoy, Dudley Dursley and Rubeus Hagrid.
VISUALISATION	Watch the movie *Harry Potter and the Sorcerer's Stone*. (Release date November, 2001.) How has the way you now visualise the principal characters changed from before you saw the movie? How do you feel about this?

From Gross, MacLeod, Drummond and Merrick (2001) *Gifted Students in Primary Schools: Differentiating the Curriculum* Sydney: GERRIC.

APPENDIX
PRO-FORMA MODELS, CHECKLISTS AND GLOSSARY OF ACRONYMS

GERRIC RESOURCES
MAKER MODIFICATIONS
SUBJECT: **STAGE:**
TOPIC:

CONTENT MODIFICATIONS	
ABSTRACTION	
COMPLEXITY	
VARIETY	
STUDY OF PEOPLE	
METHODS OF INQUIRY	
PROCESS MODIFICATIONS — *Higher-order thinking skills*	
ANALYSIS	
SYNTHESIS	
EVALUATION	

**GERRIC RESOURCES
MAKER MODIFICATIONS
PAGE 2**

PROCESS MODIFICATIONS — *Open-ended processing*	
PARADOX	
ANALOGY	
TOLERANCE FOR AMBIGUITY	
INTUITIVE EXPRESSION	
DISCOVERY	
FREEDOM OF CHOICE	
PRODUCT MODIFICATIONS	
REAL WORLD PROBLEMS	
REAL AUDIENCES	
TRANSFORMATIONS	

GERRIC RESOURCES
MAKER MODIFICATIONS MATRIX
SUBJECT: **STAGE:**
TOPIC:

	CONTENT / PROCESS		

GERRIC RESOURCES
BLOOM/KRATHWOHL ENRICHMENT MATRIX
SUBJECT: **STAGE:**
TOPIC:

CONTENT			

GERRIC RESOURCES
KAPLAN C-P-PR GRID
SUBJECT: **STAGE:**
TOPIC:

THEME	BASIC SKILL	RESEARCH SKILL	PRODUCTIVE SKILL	PRODUCT

ARTICULATING ACTIVITY
Logical sequence of teaching this learning experience, incorporating all skills and product expectations to reflect on the 'theme'

GERRIC RESOURCES
WILLIAMS MODEL MATRIX
SUBJECT: **STAGE:**
TOPIC:

PARADOX	
ATTRIBUTE LISTING	
ANALOGY	
DISCREPANCY	
PROVOCATIVE QUESTION	
EXAMPLES OF CHANGE	
EXAMPLES OF HABIT	
ORGANISED RANDOM SEARCH	
SKILLS OF SEARCH	
TOLERANCE FOR AMBIGUITY	
INTUITIVE EXPRESSION	
ADJUSTMENT TO DEVELOPMENT	
STUDY CREATIVE PROCESS	
EVALUATE SITUATIONS	
CREATIVE READING SKILLS	
CREATIVE LISTENING SKILLS	
CREATIVE WRITING SKILLS	
VISUALISATION	

GERRIC RESOURCES
GIFTED AND TALENTED CHECKLIST FOR TEACHERS
THINGS THIS CHILD HAS DONE

The following is a checklist of characteristics of gifted young children. The examples after each item are there to help you to understand that item. A child may not show all of the examples given and they may exhibit the item characteristic in ways not listed. Indicate how much you think this child is like the item by using the scale to the right of each item. Mark strongly agree (**SA**) to strongly disagree (**SD**). Fill in one circle for each item. If you are unclear or haven't noticed how this child compares to an item, fill in the **Unsure or don't know** circle. Use the space below the item for examples concerning the child, add as many details as you can remember. Be as specific as possible in describing the child's interests and accomplishments. The space is small, so please feel free to add extra pages of stories or examples to tell us more. If you can share some copies of this child's creative work, we would be delighted to have them. Use additional pages to describe anything you think is important about this child that we have not asked about.

Child's name:_____   Child's birthday:_____

Your name:_____   School name:_____

Date:_____

This child:

1. Has quick accurate recall of information.
(e.g. good short and long-term memory; quick to provide facts, details, or stories related to complex events; learns quickly and recalls accurately words to songs, poems, stories, or conversations; points out connections between ideas and events)

SA ⑩⑨⑧⑦⑥⑤④③②①⓪ SD   ○ Unsure or don't know
An example:

2. Shows intense curiosity and deeper knowledge than other children.
(e.g. asks questions incessantly once imagination has been aroused, pays close attention when learning, has an enthusiastic need to know and explore, remembers things in great detail)

SA ⑩⑨⑧⑦⑥⑤④③②①⓪ SD   ○ Unsure or don't know
An example:

3. Is empathetic, feels more deeply than do other children that age.
(e.g. exhibits maturity usually associated with older children; shows unusual hurt or pain when he or she displeases someone; displays pride in advanced accomplishments; is sensitive to others' feelings and shows distress at other children's distress or adult's distress; will subjugate their needs to the needs of others; reads body language)

SA ⑩⑨⑧⑦⑥⑤④③②①⓪ SD   ○ Unsure or don't know
An example:

© Micheal Sayler, Investigation of Talented Students, University of North Texas, Denton, TX. Permission to photocopy is granted.

4. May not always display their advanced understanding in everyday situations.
(e.g. becomes cranky or non-compliant when fatigued or stressed; playground behaviour may not reflect their verbal reasoning about the same situations; may be frustrated with their ability to meet their own high expectations)

SA ⑩ ⑨ ⑧ ⑦ ⑥ ⑤ ④ ③ ② ① ⓪ **SD**   ○ Unsure or don't know
An example:

5. Uses advanced vocabulary.
(e.g. correctly uses vocabulary and phrasings adults would expect from older children; surprises adults and children with big words or phrases they use; likes complex communication and conversations)

SA ⑩ ⑨ ⑧ ⑦ ⑥ ⑤ ④ ③ ② ① ⓪ **SD**   ○ Unsure or don't know
An example:

6. Reads, writes, or uses numbers in advanced ways.
(e.g. reads earlier than most children or if learns to read at the same time as most children, does so very quickly; likes to read rapidly to get the gist of a story even though some words are skipped or mispronounced; interest in copying or using letters, words or numbers; uses computational skills earlier than others)

SA ⑩ ⑨ ⑧ ⑦ ⑥ ⑤ ④ ③ ② ① ⓪ **SD**   ○ Unsure or don't know
An example:

7. Advanced play interests and behaviours.
(e.g. exhibits play interests that resemble those of older children; likes to play board games designed for older children, teens or adults; more apt to be interested in cooperative play, complex play situations, or sophisticated play activities)

SA ⑩ ⑨ ⑧ ⑦ ⑥ ⑤ ④ ③ ② ① ⓪ **SD**   ○ Unsure or don't know
An example:

8. Shows unusually intense interest and enjoyment when learning about new things.
(e.g. spends long periods of time exploring interesting new things; listens for long periods of time to stories and conversations; retells events and stories in great detail; entertains self for long periods of time; shows unwavering attention sometimes to the point of stubbornness; sits patiently when reading or listening to books)

SA ⑩ ⑨ ⑧ ⑦ ⑥ ⑤ ④ ③ ② ① ⓪ **SD**   ○ Unsure or don't know
An example:

© Micheal Sayler, Investigation of Talented Students, University of North Texas, Denton, TX. Permission to photocopy is granted.

9. Has an advanced sense of humour or sees incongruities as funny.
(e.g. is humorous in speech, social interactions, art or story telling; makes jokes, puns, plays on words; sees humour in situations, even ones against him or her, and laughs at the situation)

SA ⑩⑨⑧⑦⑥⑤④③②①⓪ SD   ○ Unsure or don't know
An example:

10. Understands things well enough to teach others.
(e.g. likes to play school with other children, dolls or stuffed animals; talks like an 'expert' or likes to discuss certain topics a lot; explains ideas to adults when he or she doesn't think the adult understands very well)

SA ⑩⑨⑧⑦⑥⑤④③②①⓪ SD   ○ Unsure or don't know
An example:

11. Is comfortable around older children and adults.
(e.g. craves for attention from adults; likes to be with older children and adults; listens to or joins in adult conversations; often plays with and is accepted by older children)

SA ⑩⑨⑧⑦⑥⑤④③②①⓪ SD   ○ Unsure or don't know
An example:

12. Shows leadership abilities.
(e.g. has a verbal understanding of social situations; sought out by other children for play ideas; adapts his or her own words and expectations to needs or skill level of playmates; may be seen as bossy; uses verbal skills to deal with conflicts or to influence other children)

SA ⑩⑨⑧⑦⑥⑤④③②①⓪ SD   ○ Unsure or don't know
An example:

13. Is resourceful and improvises well.
(e.g. makes ingenious or functional things from LEGO or other building toys; uses toys in unique or nontraditional ways; plays with or carries on conversations with imaginary friends; makes up believable endings to stories)

SA ⑩⑨⑧⑦⑥⑤④③②①⓪ SD   ○ Unsure or don't know
An example:

© Micheal Sayler, Investigation of Talented Students, University of North Texas, Denton, TX. Permission to photocopy is granted.

14. Shows logical and metacognitive skills in managing own learning.
(e.g. understands game rules quickly; learns from mistakes in playing games; sees errors or losses as learning experiences rather than failures; monitors difficulty of task to push self to more challenging levels)

SA ⑩⑨⑧⑦⑥⑤④③②①⓪ SD   ○ Unsure or don't know
An example:

15. Uses imaginative methods to accomplish tasks.
(e.g. presents unique arguments in order to convince others to allow him or her to do or get things; finds imaginative ways to get out of doing things they don't want to do; curious with a high energy level that is goal directed)

SA ⑩⑨⑧⑦⑥⑤④③②①⓪ SD   ○ Unsure or don't know
An example:

16. Use the rest of this page or its back to tell us anything you think is important about this child that we have not asked about. Please feel free to add any information you think might be useful in giving us a clear picture of what the child has done. Be as specific as possible in describing the child's interests and accomplishments. If you can share some copies of this child's creative work, we would be delighted to have them.

**GERRIC RESOURCES
GIFTED AND TALENTED CHECKLIST FOR PARENTS**
THINGS MY YOUNG CHILD HAS DONE

The following is a checklist of characteristics of gifted young children. The examples after each item are there to help you to understand that item. A child may not show all of the examples given and they may exhibit the item characteristic in ways not listed. Indicate how much you think your child is like the item by using the scale to the right of each item. Mark strongly agree (**SA**) to strongly disagree (**SD**). Fill in one circle for each item. If you are unclear or haven't noticed how your child compares to an item, fill in the **Unsure or don't know** circle. Use the space below the item for examples concerning your child, add as many details as you can remember. Be as specific as possible in describing your child's interests and accomplishments. The space is small, so please feel free to add extra pages of stories or examples to tell us more. If you can share some copies of your child's creative work, we would be delighted to have them. Use additional pages to describe anything you think is important about this child that we have not asked about.

Child's name:_____   Child's birthday:_____

Your name:_____   School name:_____

Date:_____

My child:

1. **Has quick accurate recall of information.**
(e.g. remembers complex happenings and describes them long afterwards in clear details; learns notes and words to songs quickly; remembers landmarks and turns on the way to familiar places)

SA ⑩⑨⑧⑦⑥⑤④③②①⓪ SD   ○ Unsure or don't know
A personal example:

2. **Shows intense curiosity and deeper knowledge than other children.**
(e.g. insatiable need to know and explore; later on he or she collects things and then learns all he or she can about them; remembers things in great detail)

SA ⑩⑨⑧⑦⑥⑤④③②①⓪ SD   ○ Unsure or don't know
A personal example:

3. **Is empathetic, feels more deeply than do other children that age.**
(e.g. feels unusual hurt or pain when he or she displeases someone; shows pride in advanced accomplishments; is sensitive to others' feelings and shows distress at other children's distress or adult's distress; will subjugate their needs to the needs of others; reads body language)

SA ⑩⑨⑧⑦⑥⑤④③②①⓪ SD   ○ Unsure or don't know
A personal example:

© Micheal Sayler, Investigation of Talented Students, University of North Texas, Denton, TX. Permission to photocopy is granted.

5. Uses advanced vocabulary.
(e.g. correctly uses vocabulary adults would expect from older children; surprises adults and children with big words they use; knows more words than other children; stops to ask about new words then remembers them and uses them correctly later)

SA ⑩ ⑨ ⑧ ⑦ ⑥ ⑤ ④ ③ ② ① ⓪ SD   ○ Unsure or don't know
A personal example:

5. Began to read, write or use numbers early.
(e.g. early interest in the alphabet and or numbers; liked to imitate writing as a toddler; copied letters, words or numbers; learned to read or count early without formal instruction; developed computational skills earlier than others)

SA ⑩ ⑨ ⑧ ⑦ ⑥ ⑤ ④ ③ ② ① ⓪ SD   ○ Unsure or don't know
A personal example and approximate age of your child at the time:

6. Understood phrases or brief sentences as an infant.
(e.g. listened intently; understood and acted on short sentences such as 'Give mum a hug' or 'Bring me the book and I will read to you')

SA ⑩ ⑨ ⑧ ⑦ ⑥ ⑤ ④ ③ ② ① ⓪ SD   ○ Unsure or don't know
A personal example and approximate age of your child at the time:

7. Began speaking first in words and sentences earlier than other children.
(e.g. spoke first words before age one; went from saying individual words to speaking in sentences quickly or, spoke first words later than age one and quickly moved to speaking in complete sentences; carried on conversations with adults as if they were peers)

SA ⑩ ⑨ ⑧ ⑦ ⑥ ⑤ ④ ③ ② ① ⓪ SD   ○ Unsure or don't know
A personal example and approximate age of your child at the time:

8. Early motor development.
(e.g. very visually attentive during the first six months, watched people carefully; followed movement intently; walked early; fed himself or herself sooner than other children; active use of toys and puzzles)

SA ⑩ ⑨ ⑧ ⑦ ⑥ ⑤ ④ ③ ② ① ⓪ SD   ○ Unsure or don't know
A personal example and approximate age of your child at the time:

© Micheal Sayler, Investigation of Talented Students, University of North Texas, Denton, TX. Permission to photocopy is granted.

9. Shows unusually intense interest and enjoyment when learning new things.
(e.g. listens for long periods of time to stories and conversations; retells events and stories in great detail; entertains self for long periods of time; shows unwavering attention sometimes to the point of stubbornness; sits patiently when reading or listening to books)

SA ⑩⑨⑧⑦⑥⑤④③②①⓪ SD ○ Unsure or don't know
A personal example:

10. Has an advanced sense of humour or sees incongruities as funny.
(e.g. is humorous in speech, social interactions, art or story telling; makes jokes, puns, plays on words)

SA ⑩⑨⑧⑦⑥⑤④③②①⓪ SD ○ Unsure or don't know
A personal example:

11. Understands things well enough to teach others.
(e.g. likes to play school with other children, dolls or stuffed animals; talks like an 'expert' or likes to discuss certain topics a lot; explains ideas to adults when he or she doesn't think the adult understands very well)

SA ⑩⑨⑧⑦⑥⑤④③②①⓪ SD ○ Unsure or don't know
A personal example:

12. Is comfortable around older children and adults.
(e.g. craves for attention from adults; likes to be with older children and adults; listens to or joins in adult conversations; likes to play board games designed for older children, teens or adults; often plays with and is accepted by older children)

SA ⑩⑨⑧⑦⑥⑤④③②①⓪ SD ○ Unsure or don't know
A personal example:

13. Shows leadership abilities.
(e.g. sought out by other children for play ideas; adapts his or her own words and expectations to needs or skill level of playmates; may be seen as bossy; uses verbal skills to deal with conflicts or to influence other children)

SA ⑩⑨⑧⑦⑥⑤④③②①⓪ SD ○ Unsure or don't know
A personal example:

© Micheal Sayler, Investigation of Talented Students, University of North Texas, Denton, TX. Permission to photocopy is granted.

14. Is resourceful and improvises well.
(e.g. finds unique or nontraditional ways; plays for long periods of time with imaginary friends; diligent in getting things they want regardless of where you've put them; makes up believable endings to stories)

SA ⑩ ⑨ ⑧ ⑦ ⑥ ⑤ ④ ③ ② ① ⓪ SD ○ Unsure or don't know
A personal example:

15. Uses imaginative methods to accomplish tasks.
(e.g. presents unique arguments in order to convince others to allow him or her to do or get things; finds imaginative ways to get out of doing things they don't want to do; curious with a high energy level that is goal directed)

SA ⑩ ⑨ ⑧ ⑦ ⑥ ⑤ ④ ③ ② ① ⓪ SD ○ Unsure or don't know
A personal example:

16. Use the rest of this page or its back to tell us anything you think is important about your child that we have not asked about. Please feel free to add any information you think might be useful in giving us a clear picture of what your child has done. Be as specific as possible in describing your child's interests and accomplishments. If you can share some copies of your child's creative work, we would be delighted to have them.

© Micheal Sayler, Investigation of Talented Students, University of North Texas, Denton, TX. Permission to photocopy is granted.

GERRIC RESOURCES
GIFTED AND TALENTED CHECKLIST FOR PARENTS
THINGS MY CHILD HAS DONE

Carefully read each of the following descriptions. Each item is followed by a series of examples; use the examples to help understand the description in the item. Decide how much you agree that your child is like the description. Mark your agreement on the scale from strongly agree (**SA**) to strongly disagree (**SD**). Fill in one circle for each item. If you are unclear or haven't noticed how your child compares to an item, fill in the **Unsure or don't know** circle. Then, tell us about a time your child did the things in the item. Try to recall specific incidents or examples about your child. Feel free to add extra pages of stories or examples to tell us more about your child.

Child's name:_____   Child's birthday:_____

Your name:_____   School name:_____

Date:_____

My child:

1. Has quick recall of information.
(e.g. immediately remembers facts, series of numbers, events, words from songs or movies, or parts of conversation heard earlier)

SA ⑩⑨⑧⑦⑥⑤④③②①⓪ SD   ○ Unsure or don't know
A personal example:

2. Knows a lot more about some topics than do other children that age.
(e.g. recounts facts about dinosaurs, sports, electronics, maths, books, animals, music, art, etc; finds out a lot about a particular subject on his or her own)

SA ⑩⑨⑧⑦⑥⑤④③②①⓪ SD   ○ Unsure or don't know
A personal example:

3. Uses advanced vocabulary.
(e.g. surprises older children and adults with the big words used; uses words unusual for a child, knows the correct terms, exact words or labels for things; acts and speaks like a grown-up when talking to adults; uses simpler words when talking to peers or younger children)

SA ⑩⑨⑧⑦⑥⑤④③②①⓪ SD   ○ Unsure or don't know
A personal example:

© Micheal Sayler, Investigation of Talented Students, University of North Texas, Denton, TX. Permission to photocopy is granted.

4. Began to read or write early.
(e.g. said or could read individual words at a very young age; started to read before entering school; likes to write or tell stories; learned to read without being taught)

SA ⑩ ⑨ ⑧ ⑦ ⑥ ⑤ ④ ③ ② ① ⓪ SD   ○ Unsure or don't know
A personal example and age of child at the time:

5. Shows unusually intense interest and enjoyment when learning about new things.
(e.g. has lots of energy and interest when learning; frequently and persistently asks how and why questions; is not satisfied with simple answers; wants to know details; loves how-to-do-it and nonfiction books)

SA ⑩ ⑨ ⑧ ⑦ ⑥ ⑤ ④ ③ ② ① ⓪ SD   ○ Unsure or don't know
A personal example:

6. Understands things well enough to teach others.
(e.g. teaches other children how to do things; explains things so that others can understand; explains areas of interest to adults)

SA ⑩ ⑨ ⑧ ⑦ ⑥ ⑤ ④ ③ ② ① ⓪ SD   ○ Unsure or don't know
A personal example:

7. Is comfortable around adults.
(e.g. spends time with and talks to adults who visit the house; likes the company of adults; enjoys talking with adults; understands adult humour and creates funny sayings or jokes adults can appreciate)

SA ⑩ ⑨ ⑧ ⑦ ⑥ ⑤ ④ ③ ② ① ⓪ SD   ○ Unsure or don't know
A personal example:

8. Shows leadership abilities
(e.g. other children ask my child for help; organises games and activities for self or others; makes up the rules and directs group activities; may be bossy)

SA ⑩ ⑨ ⑧ ⑦ ⑥ ⑤ ④ ③ ② ① ⓪ SD   ○ Unsure or don't know
A personal example:

© Micheal Sayler, Investigation of Talented Students, University of North Texas, Denton, TX. Permission to photocopy is granted.

9. Is resourceful and improvises well.
(e.g. puts together various household objects to make inventions or solve a problem; uses unusual objects for projects; uses objects in unusual ways; makes 'something out of nothing')

SA ⑩⑨⑧⑦⑥⑤④③②①⓪ SD   ○ Unsure or don't know

A personal example:

10. Uses imaginative methods to accomplish tasks.
(e.g. makes creative short cuts; doesn't always follow the rules; good at finding creative ways to get out of work)

SA ⑩⑨⑧⑦⑥⑤④③②①⓪ SD   ○ Unsure or don't know

A personal example:

11. Use the rest of this page or its back to tell us anything you think is important about your child that we have not asked about. Please feel free to add any information you think might be useful in giving us a clear picture of what your child has done. Be as specific as possible in describing your child's interests and accomplishments. If you can share some copies of your child's creative work, we would be delighted to have them.

© Micheal Sayler, Investigation of Talented Students, University of North Texas, Denton, TX. Permission to photocopy is granted.

**GERRIC RESOURCES
GLOSSARY OF ACRONYMS**

APTS	Australian Primary Talent Search
C–P–PR Grid	Content–Process–Product Grid
GERRIC	Gifted Education Research, Resource and Information Centre
HSIE	Human Society and Its Environment
IEP	Individual Educational Program
ISP	Independent Study Project
PD, H & PE	Personal Development, Health and Physical Education
PMI	Plus, Minus and Interesting
SMPY	Study of Mathematically Precocious Youth
SOSE	Studies of Society and the Environment

REFERENCES

REFERENCES

Baska, L. (1989). Characteristics and needs of the gifted. In J.F. Feldhusen, J. VanTassel-Baska and K. Seeley (Eds.). *Excellence in educating the gifted* (pp. 15–28). Denver: Love.

Betts, (1986). *Autonomous Learner Model for Gifted and Talented.* Greeley, CO: Autonomous Learning Publications.

Bloom, B.S. (1956). *Taxonomy of educational objectives: The classification of educational goals. Handbook I: Cognitive domain.* New York: Longmans, Green & Co.

Carrington, N. (1993). Australian adolescent attitudes towards academic brilliance. *Australasian Journal of Gifted Education, 2(2),* 10–15.

Carroll, H.A. (1940). *Genius in the making.* New York: McGraw-Hill.

Chall, J.S. and Conrad, S.C. (1991). *Should textbooks challenge students? The case for easier or harder textbooks.* New York: Teachers College Press.

Ciha, T.E., Harris, T.E., Hoffman, C. and Potter, M.W. (1974). Parents as identifiers of giftedness, ignored but accurate. *Gifted Child Quarterly, 18,* 191–195.

Clark, B. (1983). *Growing up gifted.* Columbus, OH: Charles E. Merrill.

Cullinan, B.E. (1987). *Children's literature in the reading programme.* Newark, Del: International Reading Association.

de Bono, E. (1992). *Serious Creativity.* NY: HarperBusiness.

DeHann, R.G. and Havighurst, R.J. (1957). *Educating the gifted.* Chicago: University of Chicago Press.

Flanders, J.R. (1987). How much of the content in mathematics textbooks is new? *Arithmetic Teacher, 35,* 18–23.

Gagné, F. (1985). Giftedness and talent: Reexamining a reexamination of the definitions. *Gifted Child Quarterly, 29(3),* 103–112.

Gagné, F. (1995). The differentiated nature of giftedness and talent: A model and its impact on the technical vocabulary of gifted and talented education. *Roeper Review, 18(2),* 103–111.

Gallagher J.J. (1975). *Teaching the gifted child* (2nd Ed.). Boston: Allyn & Bacon, Inc.

Gardner, H. (1983). *Frames of mind: The theory of multiple intelligences.* New York: Basic Books.

Gross, M.U.M. (1992). The early development of three profoundly gifted boys of IQ 200. In P.S. Klein and A.J. Tannenbaum (Eds.). *To be young and gifted* (pp. 94–138). New Jersey: Ablex.

Gross, M.U.M. (1993). *Exceptionally gifted children.* London: Routledge.

Gross, M.U.M. (1994). The highly gifted: Their nature and needs. In J.B. Hansen and S.M. Hoover (Eds.). *Talent development: Theories and practice* (pp. 45–68). Dubuque, Iowa: Kendall/Hunt Publishing Company.

Gross, M.U.M. (1994). Planning defensible programs for gifted and talented students: Rejecting the myths, accepting the realities. Paper presented at Gifted Education Seminar, The University of New South Wales. October, 1994.

Gross, M.U.M. (1998a). Issues in assessing the highly gifted. *Understanding Our Gifted, 10(2),* 3–8.

Gross, M.U.M. (1998b). The "Me" behind the mask: Intellectually gifted students and the search for identity. *Roeper Review, 20(3),* 167–174.

Gross, M.U.M. (1999). Small poppies: Highly gifted children in the early years. *Roeper Review, 21(3),* 207–214.

Halstead, J.W. (1988). *Guiding gifted readers from pre-school through high school.* Columbus, Ohio: Ohio Psychology Publishing Company.

Hansen, J.B. and Hoover, S.M. (1994). *Talent development: Theories and practice.* Kendall Hunt: New York.

Harrison, C. (1998). *Giftedness in early childhood* (2nd Ed.). Sydney: Gifted Education, Research, Resource and Information Centre, The University of New South Wales.

Hollingworth, L.S. (1926). *Gifted children: Their nature and nurture.* New York: Macmillan.

Hollingworth, L.S. (1942). *Children above IQ 180.* New York: World Books.

Hollingworth, L.S., Garrison, C.G. and Burke, A. (1917). The psychology of a prodigious child. *Journal of Applied Psychology, 1(2),* 101–110.

Jacobs, J.C. (1971). Effectiveness of teacher and parent identification of gifted children as a function of school level. *Psychology in the Schools, 8,* 140–142.

Jarrell, R. H. and Borland, J.H. (1990). The research base for Renzulli's Three Ring Conception of Giftedness. *Journal for the Education on the Gifted, 13(4),* 288–308.

Jersild, A.T. (1960). *Child Psychology.* Hemel-Hempstead: Prentice-Hall.

Kaplan, S.N. (1974). *Providing programs for the gifted and talented: A handbook.* Ventura, California: Office of the Ventura Superintendent of Schools.

Kaplan, S.N. (1986). The grid: A model to construct differentiated curriculum for the gifted. In J.S. Renzulli (Ed.). *Systems and models for developing programs for the gifted and talented* (pp. 180–193). Mansfield Center, CT: Creative Learning Press.

Kohlberg, L. (1971). Stages of moral development as the basis for moral education. In C.M. Beck, B.S. Crittenden and E.V. Sullivan (Eds.). *Moral education: Interdisciplinary approaches* (pp. 23–92). New York: Newman Press.

Kolloff, M.B. (1985). *Reading preferences of gifted students.* Unpublished manuscript.

Krathwohl, D.R., Bloom, B.S. and Masia, B.B. (1964). *Taxonomy of educational objectives: The classification of educational goals. Handbook II: Affective domain.* New York: David McKay Co.

Louis, B. and Lewis, M. (1992). Parental beliefs about giftedness in young children and their relation to actual ability level. *Gifted Child Quarterly, 31(4),* 161–164.

Lovecky, D.V. (1986). Can you hear the flowers singing? Issues for gifted adults. *Journal of Counseling and Development, 64,* 590–592.

Maker, C.J. (1982). *Curriculum development for the gifted.* Austin, TX: PRO-ED.

Marland, S.P. (1972). *Education of the gifted and talented, Volume 1: A report to the Congress of the United States by the U.S. Commissioner of Education.* Washington D.C.: U.S. Government Printing Office.

Morelock, M.J. (1994). *The profoundly gifted child in the family context: Families with children above 200 IQ.* Unpublished doctoral dissertation, Tufts University.

Passow, A.H. (1982). *Differentiated curricula for the gifted/talented.* Committee Report to the National/State Leadership Training Institute on the Gifted and Talented. Ventura County, CA: Office of the Superintendent of Schools.

Passow, A. H. (1988). School, university, and museum cooperation in identifying and nurturing potential scientists. In P.F. Brandwein and A.H. Passow (Eds.). *Gifted young in science: Potential through performance* (pp. 243–253). Washington, DC: National Teachers Association.

Passow, A.H. (1988), The educating and schooling of the community artisans in science. In P.F. Brandwein and A.H. Passow (Eds.). *Gifted young in science: Potential through performance* (pp. 27–38). Washington, DC: National Teachers Association.

Reis, S.M., Burns, D.E. and Renzulli, J.S. (1992). *Curriculum compacting: The complete guide to modifying the regular curriculum for high ability students.* Mansfield Center, CT: Creative Learning Press.

Renzulli, J.S. (1978). What makes giftedness? Reexamining a definition. *Phi Delta Kappan, 60,* 180–184, 261.

Robinson, N.M. (1987). The early development of precocity. *Gifted Child Quarterly, 31(4),* 161–164.

Robinson, N. M. (1993). *Parenting the very young, gifted child.* Storrs, CT: The National Research Center on the Gifted and Talented, University of Connecticut.

■ REFERENCES

Robinson, N.M. and Robinson, H. (1992). The use of standardized tests with young children. In P.N. Klein and A.J. Tannenbaum (Eds.). *To be young and gifted* (pp. 141–170). New Jersey: Ablex.

Rogers, K.B. (1991). *The relationship of grouping practices to the education of the gifted and talented learner.* Connecticut: National Research Center on the Gifted and Talented.

Schlicter, C.L. (1986). Applying the multiple talent approach in mainstream and gifted programs. In J.S. Renzulli (Ed.). *Systems and models for developing programs for the gifted and talented* (pp. 352–389). Mansfield Center, CT: Creative Learning Press.

Silverman, L.K. (1989). Reclaiming lost giftedness in girls. *Understanding our Gifted, 5,* 17–18.

Silverman, L.K. (1993). *Counselling the Gifted and Talented.* Denver, Colorado: Love Publishing

Silverman, L.K. (1998). Personality and learning styles of gifted children. In J. VanTassel-Baska (Ed.). *Excellence in educating gifted and talented learners* (3rd Ed.) 29–65. Denver, CO: Love Publishing Company.

Silverman, L.K and Kearney, K. (1989). Parents of the extraordinarily gifted. *Advanced Development, 1,* 1–10.

Smutney, J.F. (1995). Early gifts, early school recognition. *Understanding Our Gifted, 7(3),* 1, 13–16.

Staines, J.W. and Mitchell, M.J. (1982). *You and your toddler: The second year.* Melbourne, Australia: Oxford University Press.

Starko, A.J. (1986). *It's about time: Inservice strategies for curriculum compacting.* Mansfield Center, CT: Creative Learning Press, Inc.

Starko, A.J. and Schack, G.D. (1994). *Looking for Data: In All the Right Places.* Melbourne: Hawker Brownlow Education.

Taba, H. (1964). *Thinking in elementary school children* (U.S.O.E. Cooperative Research Project No. 2404). San Francisco: San Francisco State College.

Tannenbaum, A.J. (1962). *Adolescent attitudes towards academic brilliance.* New York:Teachers College Press.

Tannenbaum, A.J. (1983). *Gifted children: Psychological and educational perspectives.* New York: Macmillan.

Tannenbaum, A.J. (1986). Giftedness: A psychosocial approach. In R.J. Sternberg and J.E. Davidson (Eds.). *Conceptions of giftedness* (pp. 21–52). New York: Cambridge University Press.

Tannenbaum, A.J. (1988). *Myths and misconceptions in the education of the gifted.* Paper presented at Conference of the South Australian Association for Gifted and Talented Children, Adelaide, South Australia, April 24.

Tannenbaum, A.J. (1992). Early signs of giftedness: Research and commentary. *Journal for the Education of the Gifted, 15,* 104–133.

Taylor, C.W. (1986). Cultivating simultaneous student growth in both multiple creative talents and knowledge. In J.S. Renzulli (Ed.). *Systems and models for developing programs for the gifted and talented* (pp. 307–351). Mansfield Center, CT: Creative Learning Press.

Terman, L.M. (1926). *Genetic studies of genius (Vol. 1) Mental and physical traits of a thousand gifted children.* Stanford, CA: Stanford University Press.

Torrance, E.P. (1965). *Rewarding creative behavior.* Englewood Cliffs, N.J.: Prentice-Hall, Inc.

Treffinger, D.J. (1986). Fostering effective, independent learning through individualized programming. In J.S. Renzulli (Ed.). *Systems and models for developing programs for the gifted and talented* (pp. 429–460). Mansfield Center, CT: Creative Learning Press.

Treffinger, D.J., Hohn, R.L. and Feldhusen, J.F. (1989). *Reach each you teach*. Buffalo, New York: D.O.K. Publishers.

VanTassel-Baska, J. (1988). Curriculum for the gifted: Theory, research and practice. In J. VanTassel-Baska, J. Feldhusen, K. Seeley, G. Wheatley, L. Silverman and W. Foster (Eds.). *Comprehensive curriculum for gifted learners* (pp. 1–19). Boston, MA: Allyn and Bacon.

VanTassel-Baska, J. (1993). *Comprehensive curriculum planning for gifted learners*. Boston, MA: Allyn and Bacon.

VanTassel-Baska, J. (1993). Theory and research on curriculum development for the gifted. In K. Heller, F. Monk and A.H. Passow (Eds.). *International handbook of research and development of giftedness and talent* (pp. 365–386). London: Pergamon Press.

VanTassel-Baska, J. (1996). The process of talent development. In J. VanTassel-Baska, D.T. Johnson and L.N. Boyce (Eds.). *Developing verbal talent* (pp. 3–22). Boston, MA: Allyn and Bacon.

Winebrenner, S. (1992). *Teaching gifted kids in the regular classroom*. Minneapolis, MN: Free Spirit.

Winner, E. (1996). *Gifted children: Myths and realities*. New York: Basic Books.

Witty, P. (1940). A genetic study of 50 gifted children. In G.M. Whipple (Ed.). *Intelligence: Its nature and nurture* (pp. 401–409). 39th Yearbook of the National Society for the Study of Education.

GERRIC RESOURCES CONTACTS

Associations and organisations which provide regular publications, organise conferences, organise activity programs and provide a network of support to gifted children, parents, families and teachers:

National
Gifted Education Research, Resource and Information Centre (GERRIC)
The University of New South Wales, UNSW Sydney NSW 2052
Telephone: 02 9385 1972 or toll free: 1800 626 824
Web: www.arts.unsw.edu.au/gerric

National
Australian Association for the Education of the Gifted and Talented
PO Box 1213,
Strathfield, NSW 2135

New South Wales
NSW Association for Gifted and Talented Children Inc.
2–8 Grand Avenue, Westmead, NSW 2145
Telephone: 02 9633 5399
Web: www.nswagtc.org.au

Victoria
Victorian Association for Gifted and Talented Children Inc.
PO Box 184, Mulgrave, Vic. 3170
Telephone: 03 9486 9888

Queensland
Queensland Association for Gifted and Talented Children Inc.
282 Stafford Road, Stafford, Qld. 4053
Telephone: 07 3352 4288
Web: http://users.bit.net.au/~qagtcinc

South Australia
Gifted and Talented Association of South Australia Inc.
PO Box 1, Highgate, SA 5063
Telephone: 08 8373 0500

Tasmania
Tasmanian Association for the Gifted Inc.
PO Box 1942, Hobart, Tas. 7001
Telephone: 03 6227 9769
Web: www.neat.tas.edu.au/tasgifted/

Western Australia
Gifted and Talented Children's Association of Western Australia
C/- Merralinga Young Children's Foundation
1186 Hay Street, West Perth, WA 6005
Telephone: 09 8321 4821

Northern Territory
Northern Territory Association for the Education of the Gifted and Talented
PO Box 41852, Casuarina, NT 0811
Telephone: 08 8928 1083
Web: www.ntu.edu.au/local/ntaegt/index.htm

Australian Capital Territory
ACT Association for Gifted and Talented Children Inc.
PO Box 99, Lyneham, ACT 2602